ARTS & CRAFTS

Designs for the Home

DOUGLAS CONGDON-MARTIN

Schiffer Publishing Ltd

4880 Lower Valley Road, Atglen, PA 19310 USA

Library of Congress Cataloging-in-Publication Data

Congdon-Martin, Douglas.
Arts & crafts : design for the home / Douglas Congdon-Martin.
p. cm.
ISBN 0-7643-1178-6
1. Decorative arts--United States. 2. Interior decoration--United States. I. Title: Arts and crafts. II. Title.
NK805 .C658 2001
745--dc21
00-012125

Designed by Bonnie M. Hensley
Cover design by Bruce M. Waters
Type set in Desdemona//Aldine 401 BT

ISBN: 0-7643-1178-6
Printed in China
1 2 3 4

Published by Schiffer Publishing Ltd.
4880 Lower Valley Road
Atglen, PA 19310
Phone: (610) 593-1777; Fax: (610) 593-2002
E-mail: Schifferbk@aol.com
Please visit our web site catalog at
www.schifferbooks.com

This book may be purchased from the publisher.
Include $3.95 for shipping. Please try your bookstore first. You may write for a free catalog.
We are always looking for people to write books on new and related subjects. If you have an idea for a book please contact us at the Atglen, PA address.

In Europe, Schiffer books are distributed by
Bushwood Books
6 Marksbury Avenue, Kew Gardens
Surrey TW9 4JF England
Phone: 44 (0) 20-8392-8585; Fax: 44 (0) 20-8392-9876
E-mail: Bushwd@aol.com
Free postage in the UK. Europe: air mail at cost.

CONTENTS

ACKNOWLEDGMENTS

Many people have made this book possible. Indeed without the generosity of several people there would be no book at all. Each of the contributors is given a credit line with the photographs, but I would like to thank them here. Those who contributed to the antiques section of the book by allowing me access to their shops include:

- Bob Berman of the Berman Gallery, Philadelphia (www.bermangallery.com)
- Seth Carter of Olde City Mission, Philadelphia (www. oldcitymission. com),
- Pearce Fox of Pearce Fox Decorative Arts, Philadelphia (www.foxmission.com)
- Jill and Jim West of Circa 1910 Antiques, Los Angeles (www.circa1910antiques.com)
- John Levitties of John Alexander Ltd. in Philadelphia (www.johnalexanderltd.com).

Two auction houses participated by provided images from recent auctions. Thanks to:

- Jerry Cohen and John Fontaine of Craftsman Auctions, Putnam, Connecticut and Pittsfield, Massachusetts (www.artsncrafts.com)
- David Rago of Rago Auction Galleries, Lambertville, New Jersey (www.ragoarts.com).

I very much wanted to show how the Arts & Crafts vision is continuing into the present day. My purpose was to provide a sampling of what is happening in the contemporary world, which means that many fine crafts people are not included. Most of those craftspeople I spoke with were enthusiastic about the project and provided the images seen in this section of the book.

The craftspeople and other merchants who contributed include:

- Dennis and Denise Blankemeyer, whose American Furnishings

Co. in Columbus, Ohio, features many of the artists and who use their work in the wonderful interior design they create, were most helpful. Their website is: www. americanfurnishingsco. com.

- David B. Hellman, David B. Hellman and Associates, Watertown, Massachusetts (www. dbhellman. com).
- J.G. Huston and Sons (888-902-9977).
- Craig McIlwain, Black Swamp Hand Craft, Maumee, Ohio (members. aol. com/blackswmp).
- Flat Rock Furniture, Waldron, Indiana (www.flatrockhickory.com).
- Probst Furniture Makers, Hamlin, West Virginia (www.probstfurniture.com).
- John Lomas, Cotswold Furniture Makers, Whitig, Vermont (www.cotswoldfurniture.com).
- Walter Jaeger, Jaeger & Ernst, Barboursville, Virginia (www.jaegerandernst.com).
- David E. Berman, Trustworth Studios, Plymouth, Massachusetts (www.trustworth.com)
- Michael Ashford, Evergreen Studios, Olympia, Washington (www.evergreenstudios.com).
- Cherry Tree Design (www.cherrytreedesign.com).
- Mica Lamps, Glendale, California (www.micalamps.com).
- Jerome Venneman, Jerome Venneman Pottery, Oakland, California (venneman@wenet.net).
- Karim and Nawal Motawi, Motawi Tileworks, Ann Arbor, Michigan (www. motawi. com).
- Kevin Hicks, Scott Draves, Phil Eckert, and Kristin Zanetti Ephraim Faience Art Pottery, Deerfield, Wisconsin (www.ephraimpottery.com).
- Del Martin, Jax Arts & Crafts Rugs, Berea, Kentucky (www.jaxrugs.com).

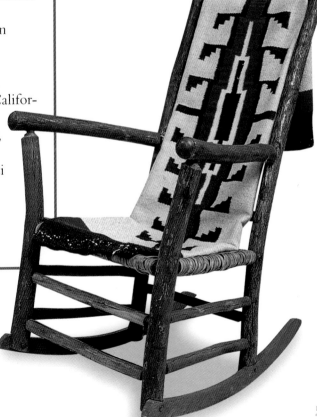

In the case of items from the various galleries represented, the prices in the antiques section are the actual asking price for the pieces shown. For auction houses I have tried to put the realized price whenever I could. The price shown does not include any buyer's premium. If the price is represented as a range, it is the pre-auction estimate.

As always prices are difficult to arrive at. Many factors affect both retail and auction prices, including geography, condition, provenance, and more. In the case of auctions a person who wants a piece may greatly influence the price on a particular day and place, the same piece bringing a completely different result at another time. Conversely, a wonderful piece can bring a dismally low price if the right person did not attend the auction that day.

The bottom line is that the buyer needs to become familiar both with the antiques and with the person who is selling them. There are reputable dealers all around the country. Seek them out...they will be your best resource!

The Arts & Crafts Movement has its roots in the tremendous cultural changes brought about by the Industrial Revolution in the mid-19th century. In England, and throughout the western world, people's lives were experiencing dramatic shifts as work moved from farm to factory, homes moved from the country to the city, and in the eyes of many the world deteriorated from a place of beauty to a place of sweat and squalor. The Movement was born as a reaction to those social upheavals and a response to new patterns of personal lifestyles that the Industrial Revolution enabled.

In the midst of the new industrial society and its stark injustices, voices were raised in protest. Karl Marx, observing the plight of the workers, published the *Communist Manifesto* in 1848. Protests led to the founding of Workingmen's Associations in London and New York in 1864.

Somewhat less radical, but at the time more influential, were the writings of John Ruskin. The British social philosopher and art critic idealized the craftsman's way of life. His influential books, *The Seven*

Armchair by M. H. Baillie Scott.
*Courtesy of the John Alexander Gallery,
photograph by Michael J. Joniec.*

The Sussex Armchair from Morris and Co. This chair was possibly designed by Philip Webb, c. 1865. Ebonized beech with rush seat, the form was often copied by other manufacturers. A Morris & Co. catalog page featuring the Sussex range quotes a biography of Morris by Prof. J.W. Mackail: "Of all the specific minor improvements in common household objects due to Morris, the rush-bottomed Sussex chair perhaps takes the first place. It was not his own invention, but was copied with trifling improvements from an old chair of village manufacture picked up in Sussex...The Morris pattern...still excels all others in simplicity and elegance of proportion." This chair was possibly designed by Philip Webb, c. 1860. Ebonized beech with rush seat. *Courtesy of the John Alexander Gallery, photograph by Michael J. Joniec.*

Lamps of Architecture (1849) and *The Stones of Venice* (1851 and 1853) formulated a vision which found acceptance in Europe and the United States, as well as in Britain. Looking back to the organization and artistic output of the Medieval Guilds as his model, Ruskin's philosophy gave rise first to the Gothic Revival of the mid-nineteenth century, and later to the Arts & Crafts Movement.

While both Marx and Ruskin responded to the changing role of the worker in an industrialized age, for Ruskin, the art critic, the secondary victim of the age was good design. Machines could be made to create ornate carvings *ad infinitum*, sending designers into a frenzy of foliage unimaginable in the former days of hand carving. At the same time, machines were limited in some of the basic areas of construction and finishing, leading designers to adapt to the needs of production rather than the needs of the consumer. He felt this resulted in designs that were excessively gaudy, without the grace and strength of well-designed cabinetmaking. Ruskin envisioned the artisan as creator who, with his own hands and basic tools, created objects that were both beautiful and useful.

William Morris, a devotee of Ruskin, embraced his model and carried it into practice. A poet, philosopher, designer and artist, Morris became the central figure in the English Arts & Crafts Movement. As a young man he journeyed to France in 1856 with his friend, Edward Coley Burne-Jones. Upon their return they both committed themselves to becoming artists. Their collaboration and friendship would continue through the years. Burne-Jones would become the most recognized artist of the Movement. Morris, who trained in architecture before turning to painting and design, was able to crystallize the principles of the movement in his design artistry and in his writings. In the 1860s he helped to found Morris, Marshall, Faulkner & Co., at Red Lion Square, London, which produced a great variety of decorative items, including tapestries, painted tiles, furniture, wallpaper, and stained glass. By the late 1870s he began to lecture about the decorative arts. An international audience was attracted to his philosophy, which presented a lively mixture of artistic and social ideals that contrasted sharply with the current state of work and creativity.

The impact of Ruskin and Morris spread across England. Study and discussion groups formed to explore their ideas, and guilds were established to enable artisans to make those ideas concrete. In May 1884 two of these organizations, the St. George Art Society and The Fifteen, joined forces to form a new society, the Art Workers' Guild. Among its members were some of the leading artists and thinkers of the English Movement: Morris, Norman Shaw, Arthur Mackmurdo, C.R. Ashbee, C.F. Voysey, Walter Crane, and Edwin Lutyens.

> The new idiom of Arts and Crafts was strong and simple in form, rich and intricate in craftsmanship, with a fresh morality based on fitness for purpose...These elements were combined in a new, eclectic style that stressed simplicity and an honesty of construction based on first-hand understanding of the materials employed...(Anscombe, *Arts & Crafts Style*, p. 54)

In 1890 Ernest Gimson, Ernest Barnsley, Sidney Barnsley, Reginald Blomfield, W.R. Lethaby, and Mervyn Macartney, all members of the St. George Art Society, founded Kenton and Co., which designed furniture for cabinet makers. It closed in 1892. Three of its members, Gimson and the Barnsleys moved to the Cotswolds in 1893 hoping to further their creativity. Others came under the influence of the Cotswold School, including Ambrose Heal, Gordon Russell, A. Romney Green, and Edward Barnsley, the son of Sidney Barnesley.

The seeds of the Arts & Crafts Movement found fertile ground in the United States, as well. During the last two decades of the nineteenth century the writings of Morris, Ruskin, and others were widely available. As in England, people organized to study these ideas further and to put them into practice. Craft societies were formed in major cities across the country. In Chicago the Industrial Art League formed in 1899. In Boston, Providence, Detroit, Chicago, and other communities large and small, Arts & Crafts societies blossomed and flourished, some of them continuing to this day. Schools were formed for the teaching of crafts. Organizations like the Saturday Evening Girls in Boston put crafts at the center of efforts to prepare young women to be self-sufficient. Hospitals used the crafts both for therapy and as a means for raising necessary funds.

It is in the context of an already thriving Arts and Crafts Movement in America that Gustav Stickley and Elbert Hubbard made their separate pilgrimages to England and William Morris. Upon his return Hubbard would establish the Roycroft Press and its associated industries near Buffalo.

Stickley started his United Crafts Guild near Syracuse, New York, producing furniture and metal wares of simple yet functional designs that he hoped would develop into an authentic American style. Like Morris Stickley lifted the ideal of the craftsman, but did not have a total abhorrence of machines, choosing instead to use them in ways that would reduce labor while having no effect on the design. This was a major factor in Stickley's successful enterprise for a decade and a half.

Another factor was his publication of *The Craftsman*, a periodical devoted to design and the Arts & Crafts Movement. While Hubbard may have been a more prolific writer, his main contribution to the philosophy of the Movement was in the advertising copy he wrote for the Roycrofters. Stickley, however, was a central figure in developing the theory behind the American movement, much as Morris had been in England. Indeed, the first issue of *The Craftsman* was devoted to William Morris's philosophy. Beyond that the magazine regularly contained articles about architecture and design, focusing on the work of major artisans around the country. It featured plans for Craftsman Homes, offering them free to readers, and suggesting designs for everything from curtains to gardens. While Stickley furniture was featured, *The Craftsman* provided various drawings and directions for the home cabinetmaker to make furniture in the Stickley style. Some have suggested that the magazine was a masterful means of promotion, and it surely was. But its impact was much broader than that; it spurred people around the nation to an understanding of good design, which was both beautiful and functional.

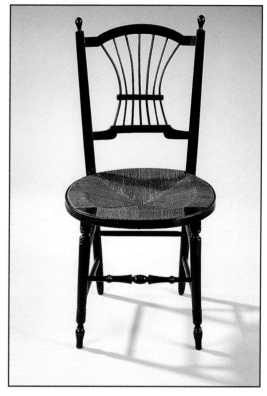

Another of the Sussex range from Morris & Co., is this "Rossetti" Armchair, so called because it is proported to have been designed by Dante Gabriel Rossetti. It is based on the designs of French country chairs of the early 19th century. Ebonized beech with rush seat. *Courtesy of John Alexander Ltd, photograph by Michael J. Joniec.*

Sideboard designed by Philip Webb for Morris & Co., ca. 1865. Walnut with brass hardware. 60" x 43" x 20.5". William Morris and Webb, an architect, knew each other from their days spent in th offices of G.E. Street. Webb designed Morris's home, Red House, which was finished in 1860. This sideboard reflects the influence of the English venacular forms, recalling furniture of the Queen Anne period. *Courtesy of John Alexander Ltd, photograph by Michael J. Joniec.*

E.G. Punnett tea table for Liberty & Co. *Courtesy of John Alexander Ltd, photograph by Michael J. Joniec.*

Armchair by E.G. Punnett for William Birch of High Wycombe, ca. 1900. Oak inlaid with ebonized wood and pewter with a rush seat. 50" x 27.5" x 18". *Courtesy of John Alexander Ltd, photograph by Michael J. Joniec.*

"Wycliff" Chair, c. 1899, by Leonard Wyburd. When Liberty & Co. opened its furnishings and decoration studio in 1883, it was under the direction of Leonard F. Wyburd. Wyburd was the child of artistic parents, and, in the *July, 1927, Liberty Lamp* magazine, was credited, along with his superior, with initiating the Art Nouveau style. *Courtesy of John Alexander Ltd, photograph by Michael J. Joniec.*

Manxman piano by M. H.
Baillie Scott for John
Broadwood & Sons, ca. 1897.
Mahogany case with copper
hardwar, 47" x 56" x 23.5". .
*Courtesy of John Alexander Ltd,
photograph by Michael J. Joniec.*

This elegant British Arts & Crafts book case is by G.M. Elwood for J.S. Henry and Co., founded by John Sollie Henry, a wholesaler and manufacturer who sold through firms like Liberty & Co. Shown here with it glass doors opened, it is of inlaid mahogany. *Courtesy of John Alexander Ltd, photograph by Michael J. Joniec.*

This Ernest Gimson ladderback armchair reflects the appreciation for and influence of indigenous designs in the Cotswold School. This chair is known at the Clissett chair, named for Philip Clissett, a Herefordshire chair bodger and turner with whom Gimson studied in 1890. *Courtesy of John Alexander Ltd, photograph by Michael J. Joniec.*

Desk and chair designed and executed by Edward Barnsley, the son of Sidney Barnsley, ca. 1925, and showing the enduring beauty and influence of the Cotswold School. *Courtesy of John Alexander Ltd, photograph by Michael J. Joniec.*

Gordon Russell sideboard for the Russell Workshop, executed by H.C. Bellman, c. 1928. 49.5" x 34" x 19". Gordon Russell began making furniture in his father's antique shop in Broadway, Worcestershire, around 1915, but his first unique designs date to early 1920s. Following the war he began designing furniture inspired by the Cotswold School, as is this sideboard. He started a shop in London in 1929, but soon faced the economic trials of the Depression. He persevered to become one of the outstanding British Modernist designers of 20th century. *Courtesy of John Alexander Ltd, photograph by Michael J. Joniec.*

Hinged settle by George Logan for Wylie and Lockhead, Glasgow. *Courtesy of John Alexander Ltd, photograph by Michael J. Joniec.*

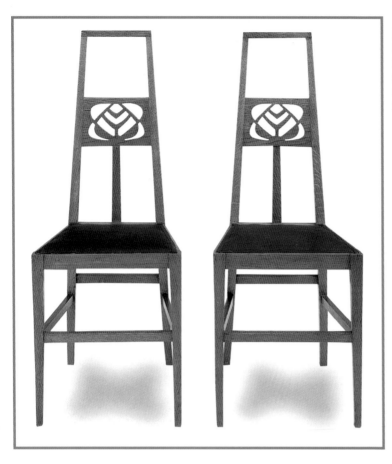

E.A. Taylor sidechairs for Wylie and Lockhead, Glasgow. A former shipyard draftsman, Taylor became a contemporary of Rennie Mackintosh, whose influence can be seen in his work. *Courtesy of John Alexander Ltd, photograph by Michael J. Joniec.*

Below: Reginald Blomfield sideboard, executed by A.H. Mason, possibly for Kenton & Co., c. 1893. Mahogany inlaid with mahogany, maple, rosewood, and more. Brass hardware. Reginald Blomfield (1856-1942) was a major force in early twentieth-century English architecture. Blomfield met Ernest Gimson, Sidney and Edward Barnsley, W.R. Lethaby and Mervyn McCartney, the group with whom he founded the early and important art-furniture manufacturing firm, Kenton & Co., in 1890. When the company disbanded in 1892, Blomfield, McCartney and Lethaby renewed their pursuit of architecture, while Gimson and the Barnsleys moved to the Cotswolds to manufacture craft furniture. The sideboard first appeared in 1893, when it appeared in the Arts and Crafts Exhibition. It was probably created under the auspices of Kenton and Co. before the break-up however. August H. Mason, who built the piece was the foreman and Kenton & Co.

The sideboard exhibited was sold during the exhibition to a Laurence W. Hodson of Compton Hall, Wolverhampton. An identical example was made for a Mr. Engel Gros of Basel, Switzerland. No record indicates whether this is the exhibited sideboard or its mate, although it matches photographs of the exhibited piece in every detail. *Courtesy of John Alexander Ltd, photograph by Michael J. Joniec.*

Ambrose Heal sideboard. Ambrose Heal, the great grandson of the founder of Heal & Sons, designed furniture for the store influenced by Gimson and the Barnsleys of the Cotswold school, his furniture began to appear in the late 1890s. *Courtesy of John Alexander Ltd, photograph by Michael J. Joniec.*

W.A.S. Benson copper and brass table lamps, c. 1890. William Arthur Smith Benson trained as an architect before meeting William Morris, who convinced him to produce turned metalwares. He opened his shop in 1880. It continued until 1920 when Benson retired. Upon Morris's death in 1896, Benson took over the management of Morris & Co. *Courtesy of John Alexander Ltd, photograph by Michael J. Joniec.*

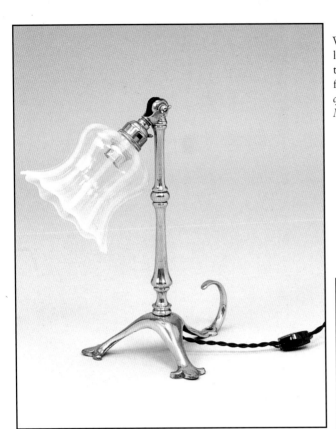

W.A.S. Benson brass sconce/desk lamp, c. 1900. 11" tall. The design of the base allowed the lamp to hang from a wall or sit on a table. *Courtesy of John Alexander Ltd, photograph by Michael J. Joniec.*

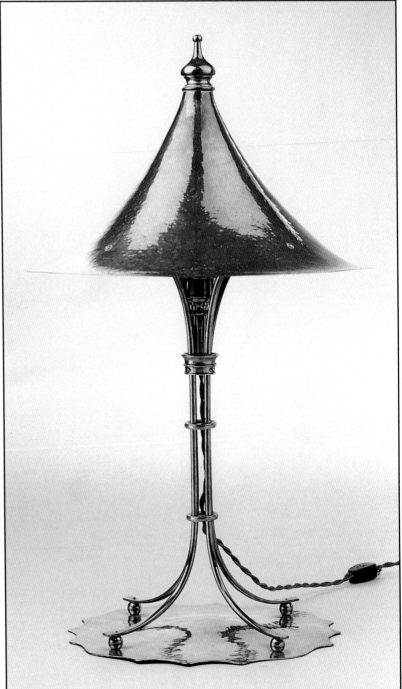

Birmingham Guild of Handicraft brass lamp. The Birmingham Guild of Handicraft began in 1890 as an expression of the ideals of Ruskin and Morris. Beginning with about 20 craftspeople, it grew to become a "limited company" in 1895. Arthur Dixon was the chief designer in copper and brass, and this lamp reflects his creativity. Other names associated with the Birmingham Guild include Montague Fordham, one of the first directors , and Claude Napier-Clavering, its first managing director and a silver designer. The firm continues today, specializing in architectural metalwork and engineering. *Courtesy of John Alexander Ltd, photograph by Michael J. Joniec.*

Christopher Dresser claret jug and mail rack. Born in Glasgow in 1843, Dresser studied at the Government School of Design. During the 1870s he designed a variety of metal wares for several British manufacturers as well as for Liberty & Co. *Courtesy of John Alexander Ltd, photograph by Michael J. Joniec.*

Oliver Baker silver tankard for Liberty & Co. Baker, an artist, was the brother-in-law and friend of William Haseler, a goldsmith and jeweler in Birmingham. The two conceived of a line of silverware in 1898. Baker produced the designs and Haseler manufactured them. In 1899 Haseler showed the work to Liberty & Co., and they were included in the Cymric range. *Courtesy of John Alexander Ltd, photograph by Michael J. Joniec.*

Large form biscuit box by Archibald Knox. Knox joined the Arthur Silver's Silver Studio in 1898. A Manxman, he studied at the Douglas School of art, where he became friends with M. H. Baillie Scott. Knox designed for the Cymric range from1899, when it was introduced, until 1911, and later for the Tudric range which began in 1901. He was the single most important designer in the Celtic revival. *Courtesy of John Alexander Ltd, photograph by Michael J. Joniec.*

In 1909 Gustav Stickley wrote that "furniture has so far remained the clearest concrete expression of the Craftsman idea." It remains so. When one thinks of the Arts & Crafts Movement, the image that comes to mind is the warm oak furniture in plain designs. Its rectilinear lines speak of a simplicity that belies its important place in the history of furniture.

Gustav Stickley became the leading spokesperson for the Movement in America, heavily influencing both the philosophy and the designs of Arts & Crafts furniture. He sought not to imitate the English Movement, which he thought produced furniture designs that were too individualistic and "showing the eccentricities of personal fancy." In his *Craftsman Homes* (p. 154) he criticized the English for furniture that was "largely for art's sake and had little to do with satisfying the plain needs of the people." Nevertheless, he shared with the English a disdain for the furniture coming out of factories. He wrote that this furniture corresponded with what architects called the "reign of terror." He compares it with the mid-Victorian period in England, which stands for "all that is ugly, artificial, and commonplace in household art."

Stickley's task was to create a new style of furniture, one that was utilitarian yet beautiful, simple yet elegant. He paid close attention to design and what is now called "ergonomics," striving for furniture that served a purpose, was friendly to its users, and pleasing to their aesthetic sensibilities. He made furniture that celebrated the ideal of the Craftsman. At the same time he made reasonable use of the latest machinery when it performed a labor saving function while not dictating the design.

The influence of Stickley can be seen almost universally among the manufacturers of furniture in the Arts & Crafts style. The result of his efforts and those of the other furniture designers and manufacturers who shared his vision is a unique American style of furniture. It represents a radical shift from the past and was a precursor of the designs that would follow in the century.

The Stickley Brothers (the first company)
Binghamton, New York, 1888-1890

The five Stickley brothers — Gustav, Albert, Charles, Leopold, and John George — were all in the business of making furniture. Gustav, Albert, and Charles went to work in their uncle, Schuyler Brandt's Binghamton, New York chair factory in 1874. In 1884 these three brothers started their own Stickley Brothers Company in Binghamton, New York. It appears that the other two brothers joined the company in 1888. They continued the company until 1890 when the brothers began separate ventures.

Gustav Stickley and
The Craftsman Workshops
Eastwood, New York, 1898-1916

After leaving the original Stickley Brothers firm, Gustav, the oldest brother, had a variety of positions, including a partnership with Elgin A. Simonds, producing reproduction furniture, and as Director of Manufacturing Operations for the New York State Prison at Auburn, where inmates produced furniture. In 1898, he made a sojourn to England where he was exposed to William Morris's Arts and Crafts philosophy and some of its practitioners, including C.F.A. Voysey. Returning to America, he established the United Crafts, in Eastwood, New York, later to be called Craftsman Workshops. A gifted designer, his furniture sought to be *"simple, durable, comfortable and fitted for the place it was to occupy and the work it had to do."*

Stickley's Craftsman furniture employed heavy structural features, including keyed tenons and chamfered boards, as well as pegged joints, forged or hammered hardware, wide chair stretchers, and flaked quartersawn oak. The forms were simple and elegant with exposed joinery and plain or leather upholstery. Stickley hired architect Harvey Ellis in 1903. Ellis, strongly influenced by his exposure to the American Southwest, produced some of Stickley's best designs between 1903 and January, 1904. These designs were lighter and revealed more grace than Stickley's. In addition, Ellis brought a strong sense of color and proportion to the work, incorporating inlaid details in metals and wood. Tragically Ellis died on January 2, 1904. His influence on Stickley's Craftsman Workshops continued.

The period following Ellis's death was an expansive time for Stickley. He bought land in New Jersey to build an Arts & Crafts community. He built the Craftsman Building in New York, a twelve-story edifice to house sales rooms and meeting spaces. In time, Craftsman furniture underwent design and manufacturing changes to conform with economic necessities, resulting in what is generally seen as a lessening of the standards of quality for which Stickley was so revered originally.

By 1915 Stickley's catalog only faintly echoed the Arts and Crafts style, being interspersed with colonial reproductions and other decorative paraphernalia. In March, 1915, the company filed for bankruptcy.

Albert and J. George Stickley:
The Stickley Brothers Company
Grand Rapids, Michigan, 1891-ca. 1940

In 1891 Albert and John George Stickley founded a new Stickley Brothers Company in Grand Rapids, Michigan. The furniture they manufactured paralleled that of Gustav, though it drew more heavily on the English Arts & Crafts Movement. Their designs were successful enough that the furniture found markets in England and Europe. Furniture was shipped unfinished from Grand Rapids to London, where it was assembled and finished.

Stickley Brothers introduced inlaid furniture in 1901, showing the artistry of Timothy Conti. Conti drew on Japanese, English, and Scottish design motifs to create some truly wonderful work.

The company used the British term for the Arts and Crafts style of furniture — *"Quaint"* — as part of its trademark. In the introduction to his 1908 catalog, Albert Stickley declares that *"Quaint Furniture in Arts and Crafts has made ideals possible which might otherwise have been impossible — has brought within the means of those with even the most modest of incomes the possibility of artistic homes."*

J. George Stickley left Albert in 1902 to join another brother, Leopold, at the Onondaga Shops, later to be called L. & J.G. Stickley. Stickley Brothers continued in business until the start of World War II, ca. 1940.

Charles Stickley
Stickley and Brandt Chair Company
Binghamton, New York, 1891-1919

Charles Stickley stayed in Binghamton, where he started the Stickley and Brandt Chair Company in December of 1891, with his uncle, Schuyler Brandt. The company offered a broad range of furniture styles, mostly period reproductions, some of which were manufactured by other firms. By 1905 they were producing a line of Arts and Crafts styled furniture, which carried the company's shopmark. Though their company outlived brother Gustav's, it, too, declared bankruptcy in 1919.

L. & J. G. Stickley Inc.
The Onondaga Shops
Fayetteville, New York, 1902-present

Leopold and John George Stickley did not have the philosophical base of their older brother Gustav, but they did share his commitment to quality. Their furniture in the Arts & Crafts style was not particularly innovative, but it was well made. They began producing furniture in Fayetteville, New York, in 1902 under the trademark of the Onondaga Shops. Their immediate success led to a rapid expansion of their business.

Never purists, they used machinery in the pursuit of well-designed quality furniture. In their 1914 catalog they wrote:

> The work of L. & J.G. Stickley, built in a scientific manner, does not attempt to follow the traditions of a bygone day. All the resources of modern invention are used as helps in constructing this thoroughly modern product, more suitable…to the house of today – your house, that is – than is the furniture of past centuries or its necessarily machine made reproductions.

The vision was to fade as the public's taste for Arts & Crafts styles waned in the 1910s. Gustav Stickley's 1915 catalog contained little of the Craftsman style. He filed for bankruptcy in 1915, and, in 1918, Leopold and John George bought controlling interest in his factory. They formed, along with Gustav and Albert, Stickley Associated Cabinetmakers, a brotherly reunion that lasted less than a year, producing some furniture with a combined label. L. & J.G. Stickley moved away from the Arts &Crafts style and introduced a line of *"Cherry Valley"* colonial reproductions. They produced their last Arts and Crafts furniture in 1923. Still in existence, they have made quality furniture in period designs since then, and in 1989 the Stickley Company reintroduced a line of Arts and Crafts furniture modeled after authentic examples of both Gustav and L. and J. G. Stickley furniture.

Charles Limbert and Company
Grand Rapids and Holland, Michigan 1894-1944

Charles P. Limbert was born in 1854 and learned the trade during the Centennial revival of 18th century designs. In 1889 he began producing chairs in Grand Rapids, Michigan, in partnership with Philip J. Klingman, an associate of Gustav Stickley. The partnership dissolved in 1892 and in 1894, Limbert formed Charles P. Limbert and Company. The company produced furniture that combined Art Nouveau and Arts and Crafts elements in a line he called the Dutch Arts and Crafts. Much of his early furniture was experimental, often incorporating elements of Art Nouveau, English Medieval, Japanese, Glasgow School, and Austrian Secession styles.

The years from 1904-1910 produced an increasingly sophisticated look, expressive of Limbert's vision. The influence of Art Nouveau gave way to other influences including Charles Rennie Mackintosh and the Glasgow School, and Josef Hoffman of Vienna. In 1906 the company moved from Grand Rapids to Holland, Michigan, and continued to grow.

Limbert introduced a new line of Arts and Crafts styled furniture in 1915. It was lighter in color and construction, and made extensive use of colored fabrics to relieve the dullness of leather's predominance. He also reintroduced a line of inlaid furniture called "Ebon-Oak" and featuring fine geometric designs of ebony inlay, sometimes combined with metals.

Limbert suffered a stroke in 1921 while on a Hawaiian vacation. He sold his holdings in the company in 1922 and died in 1924. The company however continued on until 1944.

Elbert Hubbard
The Roycroft Shops
East Aurora, New York, 1895-1938

Born in Bloomington, Illinois, in 1856, Elbert Hubbard began his business career as a soap salesman. His supplier was his cousin, Justis Weller, who was in business with John D. Larkin of Buffalo, New York. Connections were made, and in 1874 Larkin married Hubbard's sister. In 1875 Larkin formed the John D. Larkin Soap Co. with his new brother-in-law. Elbert Hubbard was the junior partner and in charge of advertising and promotion. In 1892, at the height of his success at Larkin, Elbert Hubbard sold his stock in the firm for $75,000 and retired to take up a career as a writer. A novel he had written under the pseudonym of Aspasia Hobbs, *The Man*, was published by J.S. Ogilvie & Co., New York, in 1891. After leaving Larkin, he spent the next two years writing and studying.

An admirer of John Ruskin and the English Arts & Crafts Movement, Hubbard went to England in 1894 in the hope of meeting another Ruskin devotee, William Morris, who had established Hammersmith, a community of artisans committed to the ideals of the Movement. Of particular interest to Hubbard was the Kelmscott Press. His meeting with Morris was brief, but influential. A tour of the Hammersmith community enlivened in Hubbard the desire to return to East Aurora, New York, and undertake the same grand experiment.

In 1895 Hubbard established a press at East Aurora, calling it Roycroft. He once explained that the name was coined from Roi Craft or Royal Craftsman, but it also is the name of two much admired 17th century English printers, Thomas and Samuel Roycroft. The trademark for the new enterprise was the now familiar cross and orb. The orb was divided into three sections for faith, hope, and love, to which is added an R.

The new endeavor was successful, creating a demand for new space, both for manufacturing and for the large number of visitors to East Aurora. Local carpenters were hired in 1896 to create a book bindery, followed by a leather shop, a larger print shop, and, eventually the Roycroft Inn. These same carpenters produced simple furniture for the new buildings. This furniture quickly became popular with the visitors, who often inquired where they could purchase similar pieces. Hubbard saw the opportunity for expanding his range of crafts. Roycroft furniture was born.

An early advertisement stated: *"No stock of furniture is carried — the pieces are made as ordered, and about two months will be required to fill your order. Every piece is signed by the man who made it."* Hubbard, himself, was probably never involved directly in the design or manufacture of the furniture. His realm was the world of words. The local craftsmen provided much of the original design, but over the years the furniture enterprise attracted many talented people, including Santiago Cadzow, Albert Danner, Victor Toothaker, and Herbert Buffum, all of whom contributed to Roycroft's design and production.

Hubbard, however, most certainly contributed to the promotion of the furniture crafts: His hand can be seen in the following advertisement:

> Roycroft furniture resembles that made by the old monks, in its simple beauty, its strength and its excellent workmanship. We use no nails — but are generous in the use of pegs, pins, mortises and tenons. Our furniture is made of solid wood — no veneer. We use only the best grade of quartersawed oak and African or Santo Domingo mahogany. The oak is finished in our own weathered finish, a combination of stain, filler and wax polish, that produces a satisfying and permanent effect.

Roycroft furniture is distinguished by its exceedingly high quality of materials and workmanship. The furniture is by far some of the heaviest and most massive produced in this era. The Roycrofters continued to use their heavy style to the end.

Elbert Hubbard and his wife, Alice, died when the *Lusitania* was torpedoed by a German U-boat in 1915. The Roycrofters was taken over by his son, Elbert Hubbard, Jr., and continued the traditions until 1938, when having survived the Depression, bankruptcy finally claimed this fine firm.

Oscar Onken:
The Shop of the Crafters
Cincinnati, Ohio, 1904-1931

Oscar Onken was a successful retailer in Cincinnati, Ohio. Starting in the picture frame business about 1884, he moved into the manufacture of moldings and the sale of mirrors, etchings, and artwork. While visiting the Louisiana Purchase International Exposition in 1904, Onken was impressed by the creativity shown in the Austro-Hungarian Secessionist furniture being exhibited there. In particular he was stuck by the inlaid designs of Paul Horti of Budapest. Horti received numerous awards and recognition at the Exposition for his avant-garde furniture designs. Onken introduced himself to Horti, and the two agreed that Horti would come to work for Onken designing furniture.

In a few months a new venture was born, The Shop of the Crafters, featuring Arts and Crafts furniture in oak and mahogany. Horti's inlaid designs were a prominent design element, but so, too, were design features from other Arts and Crafts manufacturers, and occasional touches of Art Nouveau and even Victorian influences. Ads appeared in the *Saturday Evening Post* for The Shop of the Crafters, promoting them as *"Makers of Arts and Crafts Furniture, Hall Clocks, Shaving Stands, Cellarettes, Smokers' Cabinets and Mission Chairs."*

Arts and Crafts furniture production had ceased by 1920, though the Oscar Onken Company remained in business until 1931.

Charles Rohlfs
Buffalo, New York, ca. 1890-ca. 1925

Charles Rohlfs entered the Cooper Union for the Advancement of Science and Art from a career as a Shakespearean actor. Around 1890 he established a shop in Buffalo, New York, and created work ranging from simple Arts & Crafts styles to more intricate Art Nouveau designs, for which he is best known. A friend of Elbert Hubbard, he was a frequent lecturer at the Roycrofters until his retirement.

Lifetime Furniture
Grand Rapids Bookcase and Chair Company
Grand Rapids, Michigan, 1911-?

A.A. Barber founded Grand Rapids Bookcase and Chair Company in 1911, a joining of two previous ventures, Grand Rapids Bookcase Company and Barber Brothers Chair Company. The company was located in a suburb of Grand Rapids, Hastings, Michigan. The Lifetime Furniture name was applied to their line of oak Arts and Crafts-style furniture. The date of the company's demise is not known.

Frank S. Harden
McConnellsville, New York, ca. 1895-1926

Founded by Frank S. Harden around 1895 its factory was in McConnellsville, New York. It closed in 1926.

J.M. Young
Camden, New York, ca. 1872-1940

There is a strong stylistic connection between J.M. Young and the Stickleys. J.M. Young was active in Camden, New York, in the late 19th and early 20th centuries.

Phoenix Chair Company
Sheboygan, Wisconsin, ca. 1875-1964
Founded in Sheboygan, Wisconsin, in 1875, by 1888 their were 400 to 500 men making furniture, mostly in oak. It continued in business until 1964. Its 1907-1908 catalog shows no examples of Arts & Crafts furniture so it is presumed that it entered this area at a later date.

Cortland Cabinet Cabinet
Cortland, New York

S. Karpen & Brothers
Chicago, Illinois, 1881-early 20th century

Oakcraft

Plail Brothers Chair Company
Wayland, New York, ca. 1900-1933
John Plail and his brother, Joseph, formed the Plail Brothers Chair Company in Wayland, New York, sometime in the early 1900s. It continued operation until 1933, despite a fire in 1914.

Quaker Craft

J.S. Ford, Johnson & Co.
Chicago, Illinois, early 20th century

Bohm Cabinet Company

Rose Valley
Rose Valley, Pennsylvania, 1901-1906
William L. Price was a Philadelphia architect smitten with the ideals of the Arts & Crafts movement. Seeking to live out the ideal of the crafts community he established the Rose Valley Association, in Rose Valley, Pennsylvania, a suburb of Philadelphia. In an abandoned textile mill he established Rose Valley Shops and set about making some beautiful, intricately carved furniture. The furniture was exhibited at St. Louis's 1904 Louisiana Purchase Exposition, but economic realities brought it to a close in 1906.

Brooks Company
Saginaw, Michigan, ca. 1910-1922
Founded by C. C. Brooks in Saginaw, Michigan, the Brooks Company began making furniture around 1910. It was bankrupt by 1922.

R.A. Macey & Co.

Derby & Kilmer Desk Company
Boston, Massachusetts, ca. 1895-early 20th century

Old Hickory
Martinsville, Indiana, 1895-1968
    Edmund Llewellyn Brown settled in Martinsville, Indiana in 1895 and went into the furniture business. He began making rustic hickory furniture which he called Old Hickory in honor of Andrew Jackson. The company stopped making hickory furniture in 1968.

Riskel

Michigan Chair & Table
Grand Rapids, Michigan, ca. 1905

Harold L. Doolittle
Pasadena, California
1883-1974
    Born in Pasadena California, Harold Lukens Doolittle was educated at Throop Institute and Cornell University where he received a degree in civil engineering. He worked for California Edison as a mechanical engineer for 30 years. He is renownedas a self-taught visual artist in many media, but particularly aquatints. His furniture making was also self taught, and reflects both an appreciation of the strong lines of the Arts & Crafts movement and a refined artist's touch at carving.

Joseph P. McHugh & Co.
The Popular Shop
New York, New York
ca. 1884-1916
    Joseph McHugh operated The Popular Shop in New York City, where he sold suitable goods to wealthy New York customers, including the latest fabrics, wallpapers, and pottery from England and Europe. These included Arts & Crafts Designs from William Morris and Liberty & Company in London. A friend sent him a chair design by Bernard Maybeck from a San Francisco church. It was a simple rectilinear design which McHugh immediately liked, and dubbed it the "mission" style. This may well be the first usage of that now popular term to describe Arts & Crafts furniture. Inspired, McHugh hired designer Walter J.H. Dudley to create a line of furniture in the "Mission" style. McHugh died in 1916 as did his company.

In *Craftsman Homes,* Gustav Stickley describes the living room as "unquestionably the most important room in the house." When Stickley wrote this the concept of the living room was relatively new, with the word itself entering the language only in the mid-1800s. Prior to this the house was broken up into small, special-purpose units; the parlor was for formal entertaining and the drawing room was for study or writing. Probably the closest space to a "living" room was the kitchen, where much of the family activity took place.

In contrast to this Stickley envisioned a "large and simply furnished living room, where the business of home life may be carried on freely and with pleasure." Instead of being divided into small rooms, he saw it as an open place that "may occupy all the space that is ordinarily partitioned into small rooms." He continued:

> It is the executive chamber of the household where the family life centers and from which radiates the indefinable home influence that shapes at last the character of the nation and the age...It is a place where work is to be done and it is also the haven of rest for the worker. It is the place where children grow and thrive and gain their first impressions of life and of the world. It is the place to which a man comes home when his day's work is done and where he expects to find himself comfortable and at ease in surroundings that are in harmony with his daily life, thought, and pursuits." (Stickley, p. 129)

The living room, said Stickley, should reflect the individuality and personality of its inhabitants. It should be designed to meet their "real needs." There were, however some basic necessities. It should have windows for exposure to sunlight and the outdoors. It needed a central focus "around which the entire place is built, decorated, and furnished." He strongly suggests a fireplace with accompanying bookcases, shelves or windows. Alternatively a beautifully designed staircase or a well-placed group of windows may do, but finally there must be one, and only one, focal point of the room.

Interestingly, Stickley suggests that most of the features such as bookcases and window seats should be part of the structure and "only such furniture as is absolutely necessary should be permitted in such a room." The furniture should be simple, use woods and colors that harmonize with the rest of the room and be arranged in a way to allow plenty of free space. The furniture should be placed in a pleasing location and left there. He cautions:

> Nothing so much disturbs the much desired home atmosphere as to make frequent changes in the disposition of the furniture so that the general aspect of the room is undergoing continual alteration...Everything should fall into place as if it had grown there before the room is pronounced complete. (Stickley, p. 136)

The living room in the Arts & Crafts ideal is the center of a broad range of family activities. The furniture that Stickley and others created for it reflect that breadth. There are pieces that bring comfort and ease to the tired worker, as well as game tables, library tables, desks, bookcases, and magazine stands. All of the furniture reflects the simple strength and elegant beauty of the Arts & Crafts Movement.

The name Morris chairs honors William Morris and an adjustable chair manufactured by Morris, Marshall, Faulkner & Co., beginning around 1866. The designer of the original chair was Philip Webb, who received the a sketch of such a chair from Warrington Taylor, who had seen it in the workshop of Ephraim Colman, a carpenter in Herstmonceux, Sussex, England. The concept translated nicely across the Atlantic. When interpreted by Gustav Stickley and others, it provided comfortable seating for the Arts and Crafts living room.

Gustav Stickley

Gustav Stickley, Morris chair, no. 332. Original finish. $8,500. *Courtesy of Craftsman Auctions.*

Gustav Stickley, early bow arm Morris chair. New finish and leather. $8,500. *Courtesy of Craftsman Auctions.*

Gustav Stickley, drop arm Morris chair no. 369. Original finish, branded signature. $12,500. *Courtesy of Craftsman Auctions.*

Gustav Stickley 3/4 Morris chair. 40" x 30" x 32.5". Circa 1905. $2,600. *Courtesy of the Berman Gallery, Philadelphia.*

Early Gustav Stickley bow Morris chair, no. 2340, circa 1902-1903. New finish and leather. 40" x 31" x 37". $7,500. *Courtesy of Craftsman Auctions.*

Gustav Stickley mahogany Morris chair. 39.5" x 30" x 32.5". $6,500. *Courtesy of Circa 1910 Antiques, Los Angeles.*

L&JG Stickley Morris chair, no. 772.
Original finish. 38" x 33" x 35".
$6,250. *Courtesy of Craftsman Auctions.*

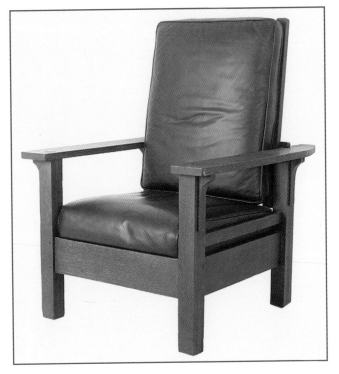

L&JG Stickley Morris chair, no. 411. Refinished, signed
Handicraft. 43" x 32" x 36". $2,600. *Courtesy of Craftsman
Auctions.*

L&JG Stickley, bent arm Morris chair.
Conserved finish. $11,000. *Courtesy of
Craftsman Auctions.*

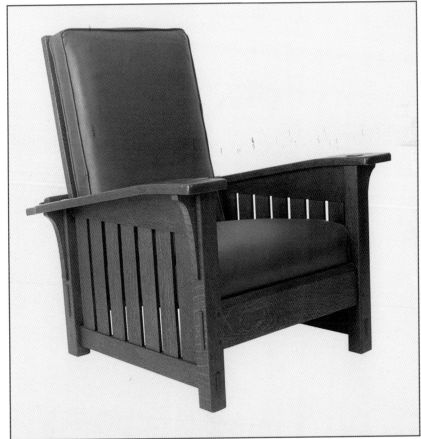

L&JG Stickley, early Onandaga Morris chair with leather and block back support. This support is a replacement. The original had a buckle so it could be more easily adjusted. $4,200. *Courtesy of the Berman Gallery, Philadelphia.*

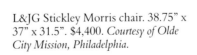

L&JG Stickley Morris chair. 38.75" x 37" x 31.5". $4,400. *Courtesy of Olde City Mission, Philadelphia.*

L&JG Stickley, paddle-arm Morris chair.
Conserved finish, "Handcraft" decal.
$8,000. *Courtesy of Craftsman Auctions.*

L&JG Stickley. *Left:* Open arm Morris chair with rope seat. Original dark finish, new
cushions. Unmarked. 41" x 32" x 36". $2,500-3,500.
Right: Cellarette with single drawer of a door. New finish. *"The Work of…"* label. 29" x
20" x 15". $3,750. *Courtesy of David Rago Auctions, Inc.*

Morris chair by Lifetime. 38.5" x 31.5" x 36.5".
$6,250. *Courtesy of Circa 1910 Antiques, Los Angeles.*

Lifetime Morris chair. 41.5" x
32.5" x 36.5". $5,200.

Morris chair by J.M. Young. 37.5" x 31.5" x 36.5". $6,500. *Courtesy of Circa 1910 Antiques, Los Angeles.*

Other

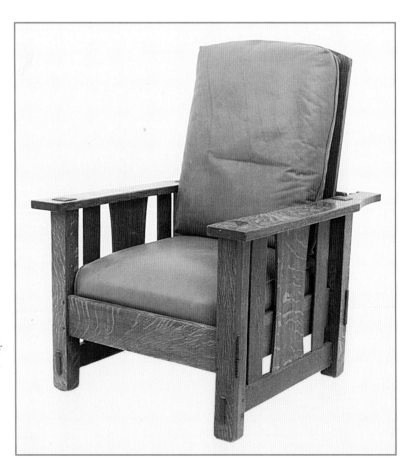

Morris chair with slat sides. Refinished. 42" x 31" x 36". $2,000. *Courtesy of Craftsman Auctions.*

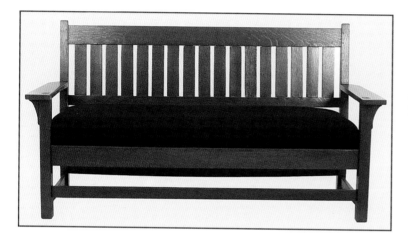

Gustav Stickley drop-arm settle, no. 219. Refinished. 38" x 72" x 26". $1,700. *Courtesy of Craftsman Auctions.*

Gustav Stickley V-back settle. 36" x 47" x 24.5". $7,500. *Courtesy of Circa 1910 Antiques, Los Angeles.*

Early Gustav Stickley settle, through-tenon construction. 35" x 40.5" x 20.5". *Courtesy of Circa 1910 Antiques, Los Angeles.*

Gustav Stickley settle no. 208. 29" x 32" x 76".
Courtesy of Circa 1910 Antiques, Los Angeles.

Gustav Stickley even-arm settle,
no. 226. 29" x 60" x 31". *Courtesy
of Circa 1910 Antiques, Los Angeles.*

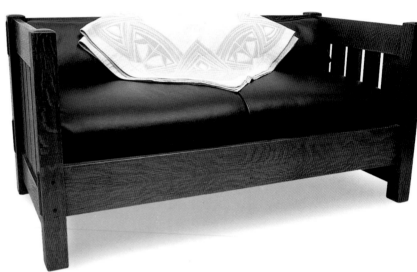

Gustav Stickley
mahogany settee, no.
165. It has tapered
posts and curved back
slats. Original finish.
41" x 61.25" x 28.5".
$17,000. *Courtesy of
David Rago Auctions, Inc.*

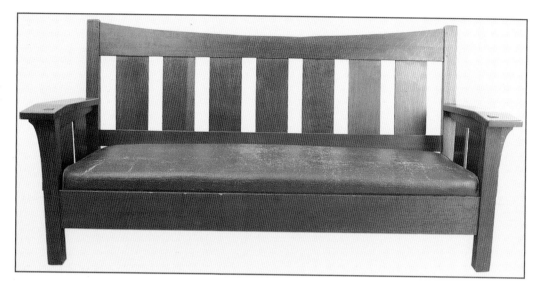

L&JG Stickley, bent arm settle, no. 263. Original condition. $7,500. *Courtesy of Craftsman Auctions.*

L&JG Stickley settle. 28.25" x 72" x 27". $4,850. *Courtesy of Olde City Mission, Philadelphia.*

L&JG Stickley settle. 36" x 53" x 22.5". $2,800. *Courtesy of Circa 1910 Antiques, Los Angeles.*

L&JG Stickley panel settle. 40" h. x 80" w. x 31.5". *Courtesy of Circa 1910 Antiques, Los Angeles.*

L&JG Stickley Onandaga V-back settle. Original finish. 38" x 51.5" x 24". $,3200. *Courtesy of the Berman Gallery, Philadelphia.*

Back: L&JG Stickley "V-back" settle with open arms. Original finish, new leather. Red handcraft decal. 38" x 76" x 26". $3,250. Front: Gustav Stickley tabouret table. Original finish on base, new finish on top. Unmarked. 16" x 14" d. $500. *Courtesy of David Rago Auctions, Inc.*

Charles Stickley even-arm settle. 33.75" x 30" x 73". $4,950. *Courtesy of Olde City Mission, Philadelphia.*

Charles Stickley settle. 35.25" x 25.5" x 58.5". $2,950. *Courtesy of Olde City Mission, Philadelphia.*

Limbert, 3/4 arm settee no. 570. Original finish, branded signature. $4,750 . *Courtesy of Craftsman Auctions.*

Limbert settee with cut-out slats under the arms. Original fish. Branded mark. 40.25" x 72" x 27". $2,750-3,750. *Courtesy of David Rago Auctions, Inc.*

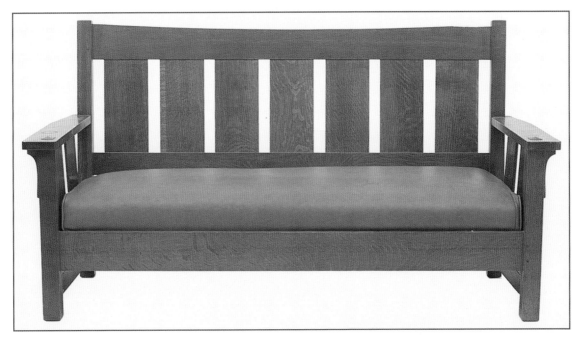

Lifetime drop arm settle with the Paine Furniture mark. Original finish. $39.5" x 75" x 29". $2,600. *Courtesy of Craftsman Auctions.*

Lifetime. Settle. 39" x 69" x 28.5". *Courtesy of the Berman Gallery, Philadelphia.*

Phoenix even arm settle. 32" x 64.5" x 27.5". $3,750. *Courtesy of the Berman Gallery, Philadelphia.*

Settle in original finish, replaced leather. 37" x 62" x 25". $1,300. *Courtesy of Craftsman Auctions.*

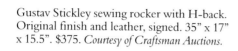

Gustav Stickley sewing rocker with H-back. Original finish and leather, signed. 35" x 17" x 15.5". $375. *Courtesy of Craftsman Auctions.*

Gustav Stickley early rocker, no. 2603. Original finish, new leather. 36" x 25" x 24". $2,100. *Courtesy of Craftsman Auctions.*

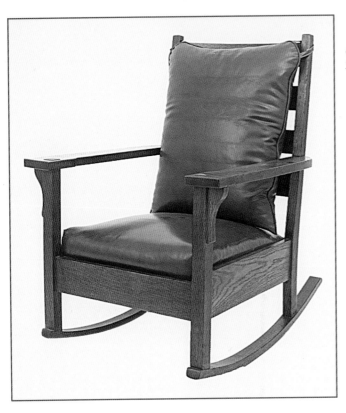

Gustav Stickley rocker. Original finish, replaced leather. Signed.
36" x 27" x 26". $1,600. *Courtesy of Craftsman Auctions.*

Gustav Stickley V-back rocker. 33.75" x 25.5" x 28.5".
$1,200. *Courtesy of Circa 1910 Antiques, Los Angeles.*

Gustav Stickley rocker, no. 319.
40.5" x 29" x 35". $3,800. *Courtesy of
Circa 1910 Antiques, Los Angeles.*

L&JG Stickley rocker. 33" x 24.5" x 27". $450. *Courtesy of Circa 1910 Antiques, Los Angeles.*

L&JG Stickley rocker. 36" x 26.5" x 29.5". *Courtesy of Circa 1910 Antiques, Los Angeles.*

L&JG Stickley. Morris reclining rocker. 37.5" x 29.5" x 35". $5,800. *Courtesy of Circa 1910 Antiques, Los Angeles.*

L&JG Stickley high-back rocker. 43.5" x 28.5" x 23".
$1,475. *Courtesy of the Berman Gallery, Philadelphia.*

L&JG Stickley tall-back rocker. 42" x 26.5" x 29". $1,750. *Courtesy of Olde City Mission, Philadelphia.*

L&JG Stickley rocker. 38" x 28" x 31". $1,250. *Courtesy of Olde City Mission, Philadelphia.*

Gustav Stickley, L&JG Stickley rocker. 36" x 26.5" x 21". $1,275. *Courtesy of the Berman Gallery, Philadelphia.*

Quaint label from Stickley Brothers. *Courtesy of Circa 1910 Antiques, Los Angeles.*

Stickley Brothers rocker, all original. 33" x 24.5" x 28". $1,200. *Courtesy of Circa 1910 Antiques, Los Angeles.*

Stickley Brothers high-back rocker. 42.5" x 25.5" x 29.5". $1,450. *Courtesy of Circa 1910 Antiques, Los Angeles.*

Stickley Brothers rocker. 35.25" x 29" x 33.25". $1,750. *Courtesy of Olde City Mission, Philadelphia.*

Charles Stickley high-back, four-slat rocking chair,
enhanced original finish. 41" x 29" x 30". $2,800.
Courtesy of Circa 1910 Antiques, Los Angeles.

Limbert

Limbert rocker. 37" x 25" x 32". $1,650. *Courtesy of
Circa 1910 Antiques, Los Angeles.*

Cortland high-back rocker. 37" x 27" x 23". $975. *Courtesy of the Berman Gallery, Philadelphia.*

Harden rocker with slat sides. 39" x 28.5" x 32". $1,800. *Courtesy of Circa 1910 Antiques, Los Angeles.*

Karpen oversized barrel rocker. A matching armchair is found elsewhere in this book. 34" x 31.5" x 28". $2,400. *Courtesy of the Berman Gallery, Philadelphia.*

A deep, slatted rocker by Karpen. 36.5" x 31.75" x 36". $3,800. *Courtesy of Circa 1910 Antiques, Los Angeles.*

Lifetime rocker. 34" x 27.25" x 31". $2,450. *Courtesy of Circa 1910 Antiques, Los Angeles.*

Oakcraft rocker. 31" x 28" x 31". $600. *Courtesy of Circa 1910 Antiques, Los Angeles.*

Plail barrel rocker. 32" x 24.5" x 28.5".
Courtesy of Olde City Mission, Philadelphia.

Rocker, possibly Phoenix.
Original finish, enhanced. 32" x
29.5" x 24". $600. *Courtesy of
Craftsman Auctions.*

Quaker Craft rocker. 32" x 27.5" x
22.5". $975. *Courtesy of the Berman
Gallery, Philadelphia.*

53

J.M. Young high-back rocker. 29"
x 21.5" x 25.5". *Courtesy of the
Berman Gallery, Philadelphia.*

Matching rocker and armchair. Rocker 33.5" x 26.75" x 29.75". Armchair 36.75"
x 27" x 20". $950 each piece. *Courtesy of Olde City Mission, Philadelphia.*

Early Gustav Stickley armchair, no. 2626. 37.5"
x 27.25" x 22.25". $4,500. *Courtesy of Circa 1910
Antiques, Los Angeles.*

Gustav Stickley V-back armchair. 38" x
25.5" x 20.5". $2,200. *Courtesy of Circa
1910 Antiques, Los Angeles.*

L&JG Stickley, early Onandaga armchair. 36.5" x 27" x 22.5". $1,100. *Courtesy of the Berman Gallery, Philadelphia.*

L&JG Stickley, armchair. Original finish. $800. *Courtesy of Craftsman Auctions.*

L&JG Stickley mahogany armchair, slatted back.
39.5" x 31" x 30". $3,800. *Courtesy of Circa 1910
Antiques, Los Angeles.*

L&JG Stickley armchair with
Handcraft label. 40" x 27.5" x 21".
$975. *Courtesy of the Berman Gallery,
Philadelphia.*

Stickley Brothers armchair. 37.5" x 27" x 20". $925. *Courtesy of the Berman Gallery, Philadelphia.*

Charles Stickley armchair with cut-outs. Original finish, signed. 37" x 29.5" x 22.5". $1,600. *Courtesy of Craftsman Auctions.*

Charles Stickley, armchair. $800-1,200. *Courtesy of Craftsman Auctions.*

Limbert, Ebon-Oak armchair. New finish, new cane. $900. *Courtesy of Craftsman Auctions.*

Limbert armchair. 38" x 26.75" x 22". $1,400. *Courtesy of Circa 1910 Antiques, Los Angeles.*

Harden armchair. 37" x 23" x 18". $500.
Courtesy of Circa 1910 Antiques, Los Angeles.

Charles Rohlfs plank
seat armchairs. One
has an original finish,
the other an old
refinish. Both are
signed. 40" x 27" x
23". $6,000. *Courtesy
of Craftsman Auctions.*

Lifetime armchair. 42" x 29" x 30.25".
$1,750. *Courtesy of Olde City Mission,
Philadelphia.*

Karpen oversized barrel armchair, a mate
to a rocker shown earlier. 32" x 31.5" x
28". $2,400. *Courtesy of the Berman Gallery,
Philadelphia.*

The Great American Chair Company armchair with Mackmurdo feet. 39.25" x 27.75" x 22.25". $1,250. *Courtesy of Olde City Mission, Philadelphia.*

Ford and Johnson wing chair. 40.5" x 28.75" x 25". $1,250. *Courtesy of Circa 1910 Antiques, Los Angeles.*

Plail barrel armchair. 32.25" x 24" x 19.5". $9,900 pair. *Courtesy of Olde City Mission, Philadelphia.*

Phoenix Chair Co. three-quarter cube armchair. 35" x 24" x 28". $975. *Courtesy of the Berman Gallery, Philadelphia.*

Grand Rapids cube chair. 32" x 30" x 26". $2,450. *Courtesy of the Berman Gallery, Philadelphia.*

Gustav Stickley

Gustav Stickley footstool. 15" x 20" x 16.25". $2,800. *Courtesy of Circa 1910 Antiques, Los Angeles.*

L&JG Stickley

L&JG Stickley footstool. 15" x 20" x 14". $550. *Courtesy of Olde City Mission, Philadelphia.*

L&JG Stickley footstool. 13" x 13.5" x 14". $1,075. *Courtesy of the Berman Gallery, Philadelphia.*

Stickley Brothers bench. 20" x 16" x 16". $775. *Courtesy of the Berman Gallery, Philadelphia.*

Limbert footstool, signed. Original finish. 15.5" x 19.75" x 14". $3,500. *Courtesy of Circa 1910 Antiques, Los Angeles.*

Roycroft "Ali Baba" bench, made of half an ash log on a keyed through-tenon trestle base of oak. Original finish. Carved orb and cross mark. $6,500. *Courtesy of David Rago Auctions, Inc.*

J.M. Young footstool. 15.5" x 20.25" x 16". $1,650. *Courtesy of Circa 1910 Antiques, Los Angeles.*

Footstool. 16" x 18.5" x 18.5". $850. *Courtesy of Circa 1910 Antiques, Los Angeles.*

Footstool with rush top. 8" x 12.5" x 12.5". *Courtesy of Olde City Mission, Philadelphia.*

Pyrographic stool. 15" x 17" x 17". *Courtesy of the Berman Gallery, Philadelphia.*

Grand Rapids window bench. 19.5" x 10" x 23". $675. *Courtesy of the Berman Gallery, Philadelphia.*

Piano bench. 21" x 35.5" x 15". *Courtesy of Olde City Mission, Philadelphia.*

Gustav Stickley lamp table. 30" x 38" d. $4,800. *Courtesy of Circa 1910 Antiques, Los Angeles.*

Gustav Stickley, chestnut lamp table. New finish, signed with "Stickley in box" red decal. $2,000. *Courtesy of Craftsman Auctions.*

Gustav Stickley tabouret. 17.75" x 16" d. $1,400. *Courtesy of Circa 1910 Antiques, Los Angeles.*

Gustav Stickley tea table. 26" x 20" d. $2,450. *Courtesy of Circa 1910 Antiques, Los Angeles.*

Gustav Stickley stand. 20" x 17.5" diameter. $1,600. *Courtesy of the Berman Gallery, Philadelphia.*

Early Gustav Stickley lamp table. 28" x 36". $2,200. *Courtesy of the Berman Gallery, Philadelphia.*

Gustav Stickley child's table. 13" x 28" x 19.5". $1,850. *Courtesy of Olde City Mission, Philadelphia.*

Gustav Stickley plant stand. 22" x 12" x 12". $1,400. *Courtesy of Circa 1910 Antiques, Los Angeles.*

Early Gustav Stickley card table, no. 447, c. 1902. It has two side drawers and through-tenon stretchers. Original finish. Early red box decal. 28.75" x 30" x 18". $20,000. *Courtesy of David Rago Auctions, Inc.*

L&JG Stickley octagonal tabouret no. 559. Original condition, signed with "Work of" decal. $1,400-1,800. *Courtesy of Craftsman Auctions.*

L&JG Stickley pedestal. 48" x 14" x 14". *Courtesy of Circa 1910 Antiques, Los Angeles.*

L&JG Stickley tabouret with octagonal top. 20" x 18". $1,450. *Courtesy of Olde City Mission, Philadelphia.*

Stickley Brothers, lamp table. $1,600. *Courtesy of Craftsman Auctions.*

Stickley Brothers telephone table with flip up top. 31" x 19.75" x 17". *Courtesy of Olde City Mission, Philadelphia.*

Stickley Brothers table. 29.25" x 26" x 20". $1,250. *Courtesy of Olde City Mission, Philadelphia.*

Stickley Brothers tabouret. 16.5" x 12" x 12". $625.
Courtesy of Olde City Mission, Philadelphia.

Stickley Brothers, lamp table with leather top.
New finish and leather. $1,350. *Courtesy of
Craftsman Auctions.*

Stickley Brothers night stand or lamp table. 39"
x 24" x 22". $2,450. *Courtesy of Olde City Mission,
Philadelphia.*

Limbert round stand with cut-out base. Original finish, branded signature. $3,250. *Courtesy of Craftsman Auctions.*

Limbert table no. 238. 26" x 15.5" d. *Courtesy of Circa 1910 Antiques, Los Angeles.*

Limbert table. 27" x 20". $1,600. *Courtesy of the Berman Gallery, Philadelphia.*

Limbert hall table. 29.25" x 30" x 22". $1,250. Olde City *Courtesy of Olde City Mission, Philadelphia.*

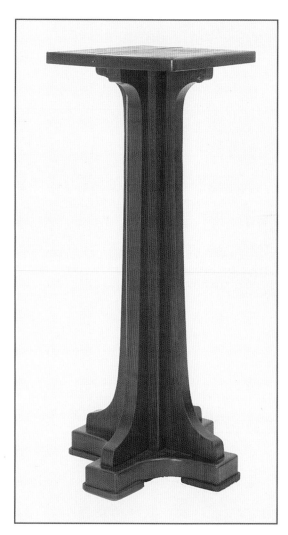

Limbert plant stand. Branded mark. $2,600. *Courtesy of Craftsman Auctions.*

Limbert four-drawer stand, no. 260, an early and rare form. Original finish, some veneer buckling on sides. Paper label only. 36" x 17" x 15.5". $2,900.

Roycroft tabouret with keyhole cut-outs.
Refinished. Carved orb and cross mark.
20.5" x 15" x 15". $4,750. *Courtesy of David
Rago Auctions, Inc.*

Card table. 29" x 36" x 36". *Courtesy of
Circa 1910 Antiques, Los Angeles.*

Grand Rapids hexagonal tabouret. 16" x 14".
$750. *Courtesy of Circa 1910 Antiques, Los Angeles.*

Stand. Bohm Cabinet Company, Rochester, New York. 29" x 16". $1,100. *Courtesy of the Berman Gallery, Philadelphia.*

Hexagonal table. 22.5" x 16.5". *Courtesy of Olde City Mission, Philadelphia.*

Mission round-top table. 30" x 20" diameter. *Courtesy of Olde City Mission, Philadelphia.*

Grand Rapids lunch table. 30" x 30" x 23.5" $1,275. *Courtesy of the Berman Gallery, Philadelphia.*

Pyrographic side tables. Left: 21" x 17"; center: 17" x 16"; right: 21" x 19.5". $675 each. *Courtesy of the Berman Gallery, Philadelphia.*

Gustav Stickley

Gustav Stickley liquor cabinet. New finish, minor repair, red decal. $2,000. *Courtesy of Craftsman Auctions.*

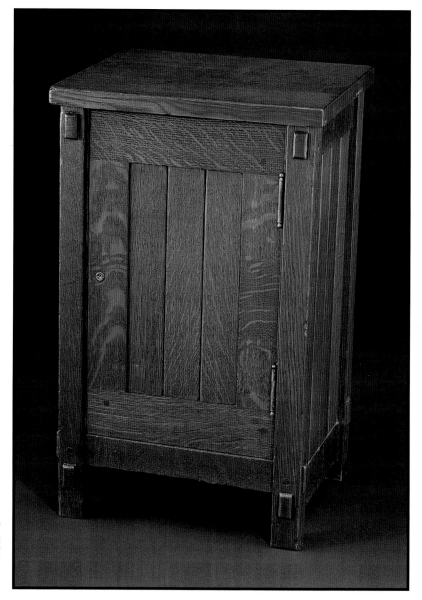

Gustav Stickley smoking cabinet with interior drawer and divided storage spaces. Top and front refinished. 27" x 17" x 15". $5,500. *Courtesy of David Rago Auctions, Inc.*

L&JG Stickley cellarette, no. 23. Original finish, signed. 36" x 32" x 16". $7,000. *Courtesy of Craftsman Auctions.*

Harden, gun case. Original finish, signed. $1,700. *Courtesy of Craftsman Auctions.*

Gustav Stickley

Gustav Stickley library table, no. 616. Original finish, red decal. $5,000. *Courtesy of Craftsman Auctions.*

Gustav Stickley 42" library table. Top refinished. Signed in drawer. 30" x 29" x 42". $2,250. *Courtesy of Olde City Mission, Philadelphia.*

Gustav Stickley small desk. 29" x 44" x 26". $1,900. *Courtesy of the Berman Gallery, Philadelphia.*

Gustav Stickley three-drawer library table. Original finish with normal light wear. Large red decal under table. 30" x 66" x 36". $25,000. *Courtesy of David Rago Auctions, Inc.*

Gustav Stickley spindle library table, no. 655. Signed. 29" x 36.25" x 24". $3,800. *Courtesy of Olde City Mission, Philadelphia.*

Gustav Stickley drop-front desk, no. 731. Branded signature on drawer, refinished with some veneer repair. 43.5" x 32" x 16". $1,300. *Courtesy of Craftsman Auctions.*

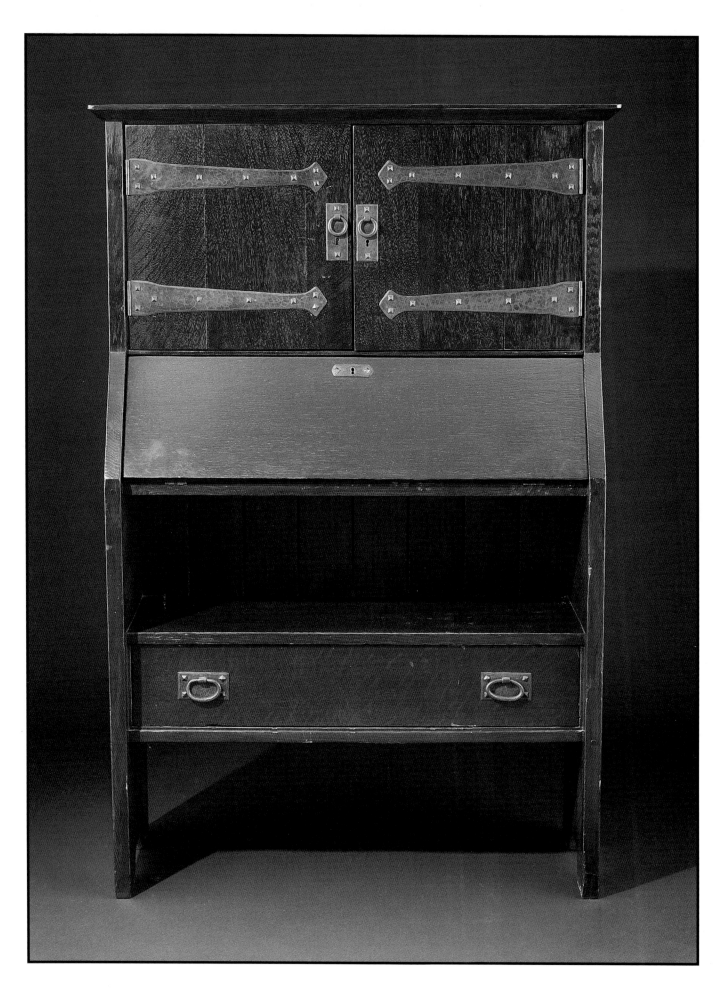

Gustav Stickley drop-front desk, c. 1901, with upper gallery cabinet. The doors have hammered copper strap hardware. New ebonized finish. Red decal. 56" x 38.25" x 15". $7,500. *Courtesy of David Rago Auctions, Inc.*

Gustav Stickley drop-front desk, no. 732, with four drawers. New finish, red decal and paper label. $1,750. *Courtesy of Craftsman Auctions.*

Gustav Stickley drop-front desk. 38.5" x 29" x 13". $3,800. *Courtesy of Circa 1910 Antiques, Los Angeles.*

Gustav Stickley drop-front desk with chamfered sides, back and front panel, through-tenon construction, and a gallery top. Original finish. Unmarked. 52" x 25.75" x 11". $15,000. *Courtesy of David Rago Auctions, Inc.*

Early Gustav Stickley circular library table, no. 636, c. 1902. Original tacked on leather top, through-tenon stretchers. Original finish. Large red box decal. 30" x 48" d. $22,500. *Courtesy of David Rago Auctions, Inc.*

Gustav Stickley hexagonal library table with
leather top. 29" h. x 48" d. $9,000. *Courtesy of
Circa 1910 Antiques, Los Angeles.*

L&JG Stickley library table. Original finish, signed. 29" x 24" x 36". $1,200. *Courtesy of Craftsman Auctions.*

L&JG Stickley desk in original finish. 29.5" x 48" x 30". $2,650. *Courtesy of the Berman Gallery, Philadelphia.*

L&JG Stickley/Onandaga Shops drop-front desk with through-tenon construction and a gallery at the top. New finish and some replacement pieces. Unmarked. 45" x 40" x 18". $1,800. *Courtesy of David Rago Auctions, Inc.*

L&JG Stickley trestle library table. 29" x 54" x 30". $4,200. *Courtesy of Circa 1910 Antiques, Los Angeles.*

Stickley Brothers library table. Refinished, Quaint tag. 29.5" x 48" x 30". $1,200. *Courtesy of Craftsman Auctions.*

Stickley Brothers library table with leather top. New finish, new leather. $1,100. *Courtesy of Craftsman Auctions.*

Stickley Brothers desk. 29.5" x 46" x 28". $1,650. *Courtesy of the Berman Gallery, Philadelphia.*

Stickley Brothers drop-front desk. Original finish. $2,100. *Courtesy of Craftsman Auctions.*

Limbert library table, no. 165. Refinished. $1,250. *Courtesy of Craftsman Auctions.*

Limbert library table, no. 146. 29" x 45" x 30". $4,900. *Courtesy of Olde City Mission, Philadelphia.*

Limbert library table with three drawers. 29" x 60" x 32". $3,200. *Courtesy of Circa 1910 Antiques, Los Angeles.*

Limbert library table with bookcase sides, no. 1128. 29.5" x 48" x 30". $1,500. *Courtesy of Craftsman Auctions.*

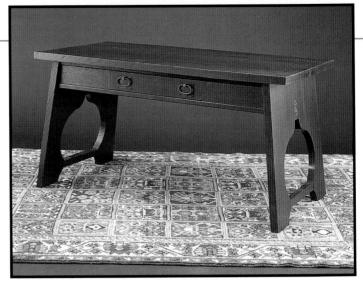

Roycroft library table in a rare form with flaring plank sides and Moorish cut-outs. New dark finish. Carved with orb and cross mark. 30" x 59.5" x 30". $9,000. *Courtesy of David Rago Auctions, Inc.*

Roycroft library table with Mackmurdo feet. Skinned finish. Carved orb and cross mark. 27.75" x 30" x 22". $4,000. *Courtesy of David Rago Auctions, Inc.*

Roycroft. *Left:* Mahogany desk chair. The hourglass back slat is carved with the letter H. Original finish. Carved orb and cross mark. 43.5" x 17" x 17". $1,400. *Right:* Mahogany writing table with slatted sides. The lower shelf has keyed through tenons. Carved orb and cross mark. 30" x 48" x 30". $5,000. The lamp on the desk is by Dirk Van Erp. It is hammered copper with a four-panel mica shade over four sockets. Original condition. Closed box mark. 19" x 21" d. $55,000. *Courtesy of David Rago Auctions, Inc.*

Ford Johnson desk. 29.25" x 40" x 24.5". $1,375. *Courtesy of the Berman Gallery, Philadelphia.*

Charles Rohlfs library table. Original finish, branded signature. 29.5" x 60" x 33". $12,500. *Courtesy of Craftsman Auctions.*

Lifetime trestle library table with leather top (replaced), no. 934. Partial paper label, original finish with minor wear. 29" x 48" x 30". $1,100. *Courtesy of Craftsman Auctions.*

Rose Valley

Rose Valley trestle library table, c. 1902. The top is butterfly-joined and the standards are carved with Gothic rose medallions. Original finish with normal wear. Marked with carved "Rose V" insignia on both sides. 29" x 48" x 35". $19,000. *Courtesy of David Rago Auctions, Inc.*

Shop of the Crafters

Shop of the Crafters drop-lid desk. 48" x 30" x 16". $1,625. *Courtesy of the Berman Gallery, Philadelphia.*

Mission desk with rattan panel. 30.25" x 48" x 28". $1,675. *Courtesy of Olde City Mission, Philadelphia. Courtesy of Olde City Mission, Philadelphia.*

Drop front desk with bookcase sides, possibly by Brooks. Refinished. 50" x 62.5" x 14". $2,000. *Courtesy of Craftsman Auctions.*

Mission desk. 42.25" x 28.5" x 21". $1,250. *Courtesy of Olde City Mission, Philadelphia.*

Gustav Stickley

Gustav Stickley. *Left:* Early lamp table with circular tip, arched apron and stretchers, and through-tenons. New finish and unmarked. 28.75" x 40" d. $4,250. *Right:* Two-door bookcase with gallery top. Original finish with some touch-up. Paper label. 56" x 48" x 13". $7,000. *Courtesy of David Rago Auctions, Inc.*

Gustav Stickley early open bookcase. Original finish. $5,750. *Courtesy of Craftsman Auctions.*

Gustav Stickley double-door bookcase designed by Harvey Ellis. New dark finish. Red decal on inside, paper label on back. 58" x 48" x 14". $12,000. *Courtesy of David Rago Auctions, Inc.*

L&JG Stickley bookcase with keyed tenons. 54" x 49" x 12". *Courtesy of Circa 1910 Antiques, Los Angeles.*

L&JG Stickley bookcase. 55" x 30" x 12". $9,800. *Courtesy of Olde City Mission, Philadelphia.*

Early L&JG Stickley triple bookcase with full gallery top and keyed
through-tenons. Original dark finish. 56.5" x 77" x 12". $13,000. *Courtesy of
David Rago Auctions, Inc.*

Stickley Brothers bookshelf. 47"
x 15.5" x 12". $1,375. *Courtesy of
the Berman Gallery, Philadelphia.*

Limbert double door bookcase, no. 358. Original finish,
signed. 58.5" x 48" x 14.5". $4,000. *Courtesy of Craftsman
Auctions.*

Limbert bookcase. 52" x 48" x 14".
$4,200. *Courtesy of Olde City Mission,
Philadelphia.*

Limbert. *Left:* Double door bookcase with heart shaped cut out and two shelves over glass doors. New finish. Paper label and branded mark. 47" x 31.5" x 11.5". $2,600. *Right:* China cabinet with corbels and raised plate rail. Overcoated original finish. 64.5" x 46.25" x 15.75". $8,000. *Courtesy of David Rago Auctions, Inc.*

Limbert bookshelf. 28" x 27.5" x 11.5". $1,375. *Courtesy of the Berman Gallery, Philadelphia.*

Lifetime double-door bookcase. Original finish, decal and paper label. $2,000. *Courtesy of Craftsman Auctions.*

Lifetime single-door bookcase. Original finish, "Paine" label. $2,000. *Courtesy of Craftsman Auctions.*

Roycroft open bookcase with bottom drawer. Original light finish. Carved orb and cross mark. 65.25" x 34" x 9.25". $6,500. *Courtesy of David Rago Auctions, Inc.*

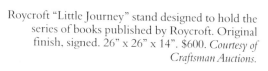

Roycroft "Little Journey" stand designed to hold the series of books published by Roycroft. Original finish, signed. 26" x 26" x 14". $600. *Courtesy of Craftsman Auctions.*

Macey four-piece stacking bookcase with glass doors. 57" x 25" x 12.75". $2,250. *Courtesy of Olde City Mission, Philadelphia.*

Macey Co. stack bookcase. $1,700. *Courtesy of Craftsman Auctions.*

Derby & Kilmer Desk Company, Boston, Massachusetts, double door bookcase. 48" x 42" x 12.5". $2,300. *Courtesy of the Berman Gallery, Philadelphia.*

Bookcase with cut-outs. Original finish. 57" x 40" x 13". $1,400. *Courtesy of Craftsman Auctions.*

Gustav Stickley

Gustav Stickley magazine stand. 34.5" x 15.25" x 15.25". $6,800. *Courtesy of Olde City Mission, Philadelphia.*

Gustav Stickley magazine stand, no. 548. Original finish with paper label and brand. 44" x 16" x 16". $3,750. *Courtesy of Craftsman Auctions.*

L&JG Stickley magazine stand. 45.25" x 12" x 18.75". $3,200. *Courtesy of Olde City Mission, Philadelphia.*

L&JG Stickley magazine stand, no. 46. Original finish, signed. $2,250. *Courtesy of Craftsman Auctions.*

Limbert magazine stand. 37" x 16.5" (flares to 20.25" at the bottom) x 10.5" (flares to 14.25" at the bottom). $1,450. *Courtesy of Olde City Mission, Philadelphia.*

Magazine stand. $600-900.
Courtesy of Craftsman Auctions.

Magazine stand. 38.5" x 18.5". $875.
Courtesy of the Berman Gallery, Philadelphia.

Mission magazine stand. 46.5" x
16" x 12". $725. *Courtesy of Olde
City Mission, Philadelphia.*

Magazine stand.
29.5" x 29.25" x 13".
$950. *Courtesy of Olde
City Mission,
Philadelphia.*

Magazine stand. 43" high. Top, 19" x 10"; bottom,
22" x 14". *Courtesy of Circa 1910 Antiques, Los Angeles.*

Gustav Stickley

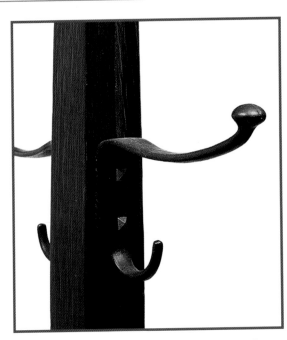

Gustav Stickley double costumer. 72" x 13" x 22". $3,800. *Courtesy of Circa 1910 Antiques, Los Angeles.*

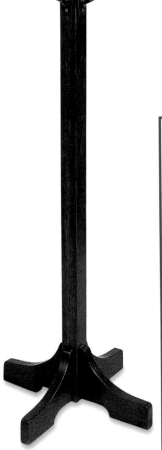

Gustav Stickley single costumer. 60" tall. $1,250. *Courtesy of the Berman Gallery, Philadelphia.*

Unusual Stickley Brothers
double costumer. 67" x 14.5".
$1,300. *Courtesy of the Berman
Gallery, Philadelphia.*

Stickley Brothers wastebasket.
17.5" x 14.25" x 14.25".
*Courtesy of Olde City Mission,
Philadelphia.*

Stickley Brothers woodholder,
no. 6, oak and copper. 19.5" x
20" x 19". $2,450. *Courtesy of
Circa 1910 Antiques, Los Angeles.*

Rohlfs, oak and copper candlestick. $750-950. *Courtesy of Craftsman Auctions.*

Ernest Batchelder blanket chest with cut-out feet and pyrographic front panel. 15" x 27.25" x 14". $8,500. *Courtesy of David Rago Auctions, Inc.*

Unusual Rose Valley swiveling pedestal carved as a miniature of King Arthur's Round Table. At the center is a rose medallion with a knight carved above it. About the circumference are the names of Arthur's knights. Original finish. 5.5" x 22" d. $2,100. *Courtesy of David Rago Auctions, Inc.*

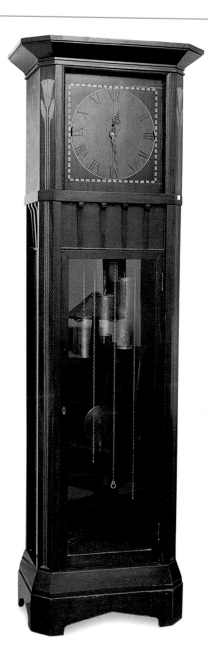

Shop of the Crafters tall Manchester clock, mahogany. 85" x 27" x 16". *Courtesy of Circa 1910 Antiques, Los Angeles.*

Shelf clock, oak with pewter face. 12.75" x 5.5" x 4.5". $1,650. *Courtesy of Circa 1910 Antiques, Los Angeles.*

Mirrored hall tree. 73.5" x 35.5" x 17". $2,500. *Courtesy of Olde City Mission, Philadelphia.*

Barber Brothers umbrella stand. 27.5" x 14.75" x 13". $950. *Courtesy of Circa 1910 Antiques, Los Angeles.*

Folding screen. 68" x 60". $750. *Courtesy of Olde City Mission, Philadelphia.*

Antique Glenmure rug designed by C.F.A. Voysey. Manufactured in Ireland, ca. 1903. 6'8" x 8'. This rug is rare or unique in this size. To achieve it the knots were tied on a single warp to fit more in, and the variant border is half as wide as on larger sizes. *Courtesy of Jax Rugs.*

Window in slag glass, c. 1901. 80" x 47". $7,000. *Courtesy of David Rago Auctions, Inc.*

Old Hickory rocker. 33" x 24.5" x 23". $950. *Courtesy of the Berman Gallery, Philadelphia.*

Old Hickory chair rocker. 31" x 24" x 18". $975. *Courtesy of the Berman Gallery, Philadelphia.*

Old Hickory rocker. 46.5" x 25" x 20". $1,100. *Courtesy of the Berman Gallery, Philadelphia.*

Old Hickory chair desk chair. 36" x 17" x 16". *Courtesy of the Berman Gallery, Philadelphia.*

Old Hickory armchair. 35.5" x 22.5" x 20.5". $950. *Courtesy of the Berman Gallery, Philadelphia.*

Old Hickory octagonal table. 29" x 24". $1,200. *Courtesy of the Berman Gallery, Philadelphia.*

Old Hickory sidechair. 38" x 20" x 16.5". Set of four: $2,400. *Courtesy of the Berman Gallery, Philadelphia.*

Stickley placed the importance of the dining room only a little lower than that of the living room. It was the center of "hospitality and good cheer, the place that should hold a special welcome for guests and home folk alike."

The dining room's design should promote two things, according to Stickley: convenience and cheerfulness. Regarding convenience, the requirements are fairly obvious: it should be near the kitchen and it should have a swinging door to keep the noise and odors of the kitchen at bay.

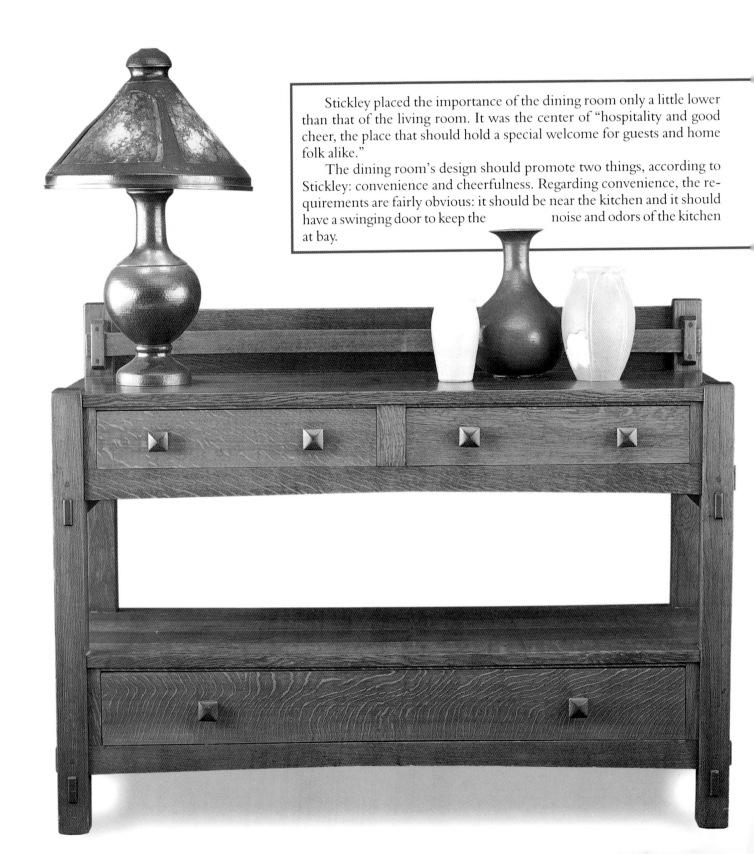

For cheerfulness exposure to sunlight is ideal, though excessive sunlight may call for a color scheme that is "cool and restful." On the other hand, if the room does not have direct sunlight the color scheme can help by adding warmth to the room.

As in the living room Stickley recommends the use of built-in features in the dining room. He also repeats his recommendation for a focal point, suggesting a built-in sideboard, a small solarium for plants or a window seat. Lacking those, one of the beautiful sideboards he and his fellow manufacturers produced would do quite nicely.

Gustav Stickley

Gustav Stickley server designed by Harvey Ellis. It has a gallery top and three drawers over a large linen drawer. Original finish and black ink mark. 40.25" x 53.5" x 18.25". $20,000. *Courtesy of David Rago Auctions, Inc.*

Gustav Stickley oversized server with plate rack and three drawers. New finish. Large red decal. 44.25" x 59.25" x 24". $14,000. *Courtesy of David Rago Auctions, Inc.*

Gustav Stickley sideboard with gallery by Harvey Ellis. Original dark chip with normal wear. Large red decal. 42" x 60" x 22.25". $13,000. *Courtesy of David Rago Auctions, Inc.*

Gustav Stickley sideboard in original finish.
Some veneer damage. 45" x 48" x 18". $2,600.
Courtesy of Craftsman Auctions.

Gustav Stickley server. 39" x 48" x 20". *Courtesy of Circa 1910
Antiques, Los Angeles.*

Gustav Stickley server. Original finish, signed. 39" x
42" x 20". $4,000. *Courtesy of Craftsman Auctions.*

Gustav Stickley sideboard, no. 814-1/2.
Original finish, branded signature.
$5,250. *Courtesy of Craftsman Auctions.*

L&JG Stickley. *Left:* Set of six ladderback dining chairs (four shown), one of which is an armchair. *"The work of…"* label. Armchair: 37" x 25.5" x 21.5". $2,800.
Right: Sideboard with plate rail, hammered copper straps, and copper pulls. Branded *"The work of…"* 45.25" x 60" x 21.75". $3,750. *Courtesy of David Rago Auctions, Inc.*

Signed Stickley Brothers sideboard with original finish. 44" x 72" x 22". *Courtesy of Circa 1910 Antiques, Los Angeles.*

Stickley Brothers server. Original finish, partial paper label. *Courtesy of Craftsman Auctions.*

Limbert sideboard with mirror. Original finish, branded mark. 54" x 54" x 20". $3,850. *Courtesy of Craftsman Auctions.*

Limbert. *Left:* Extension dining table, no. 1480-C-54, with round top. It has a central pedestal and four through-tenon legs. Skinned finish, some repair. Branded mark. Closed: 28" x 54" d. $3,250.
Right: Sideboard, no. 1453 3/4, with open plate rack on mirrored backsplash. Skinned finish. Branded mark and *1453* on back. 52" x 48" x 19". $2,600. *Courtesy of David Rago Auctions, Inc.*

Lifetime sideboard. 39.5" x 47" x 21.5". $2,600. *Courtesy of the Berman Gallery, Philadelphia.*

Riskel Furniture Co. sideboard. 35" x 42" x 19".
$1,475. *Courtesy of the Berman Gallery, Philadelphia.*

Phoenix server. 37" x 36" x 16". $1,400. *Courtesy of the Berman Gallery, Philadelphia.*

Grand Rapids sideboard. 49" x 48" x 20"
$2,100. *Courtesy of the Berman Gallery, Philadelphia.*

Gustav Stickley single-door china cabinet designed by Harvey Ellis. Original finish and glass. Unmarked. $17,000. *Courtesy of David Rago Auctions, Inc.*

L&JG Stickley

L&JG Stickley china cabinet. 70" x 47" x 16". $40,000. *Courtesy of the Berman Gallery, Philadelphia.*

Stickley Brothers two-door china cabinet.
Original finish. $4,550. *Courtesy of Craftsman Auctions.*

Stickley Brothers china cabinet, no. 8447. Original finish. 59" x 47.5" x 15.5". $6,500. *Courtesy of Craftsman Auctions.*

Stickley Brothers china cabinet. Original finish, stenciled model number. *Courtesy of Craftsman Auctions.*

Lifetime double china cabinet. 54" x 15.5" x 32". $2,200.
Courtesy of the Berman Gallery, Philadelphia.

Grand Rapids Bookcase Co. china cabinet, c. 1900.
Signed under top. 57" x 30.5" x 15". $2,100.
Courtesy of the Berman Gallery, Philadelphia.

Left: Double door chestnut and oak bookcase. Rough original finish. 54.75" x 42" x 17.75". $2,150.
Right: Lifetime double-door china cabinet with through-tenon top and gallery. Original finish and hardware. 54" x 55" x 16". $4,000. *Courtesy of David Rago Auctions, Inc.*

Gustav Stickley

Gustav Stickley round dining table no. 656 with three leaves. New finish, paper label signature. $4,950. *Courtesy of Craftsman Auctions.*

Gustav Stickley round oak table with two leaves. New finish. $2,400-2,800. *Courtesy of Craftsman Auctions.*

Gustav Stickley set of five early ladderback dining chairs, including one armchair. Original finish, reupholstered. Stickley decal. $4,250. Pedestal round dining table. Original finish, minor wear. Paper label. 30" x 54.25" d. $6,500. *Courtesy of David Rago Auctions, Inc.*

L&JG Stickley dining table with two leaves. 29.5" x 48". $3,500. *Courtesy of Olde City Mission, Philadelphia.*

Roycroft extension dining table, no. 013. It has five legs and is complete with four original leaves. Original finish on base, top refinished. 29.5" x 48" d. $7,000. *Courtesy of David Rago Auctions, Inc.*

Michigan Chair & Table Company table. 40" d. x 29". $2,600. *Courtesy of Circa 1910 Antiques, Los Angeles.*

Gustav Stickley

Gustav Stickley sidechair and armchair, no. 306 1/2. Armchair: 35.5" x 24.75" x 20.5". Sidechair: 35.5" x 17" x 16.5". Set of five sidechairs and an armchair $4,500. *Courtesy of Circa 1910 Antiques, Los Angeles.*

Gustav Stickley dining room armchairs. Enhanced original finish, replaced leather. Signed. 37" x 26.5" x 22". Set of eight, $7,200. *Courtesy of Craftsman Auctions.*

Gustav Stickley H-back dining chairs. Refinished, branded mark. $3,000-3,500 for the set of six. *Courtesy of Craftsman Auctions.*

L&JG Stickley armchairs and sidechairs, nos. 820 and 822. The chairs have their original finish though the sidechairs' finishes have been enchanced; the leather is replaced. Armchairs: 36" x 27" x 20.5"; sidechairs: 36" x 20" x 17". $3,100 for four. *Courtesy of Craftsman Auctions.*

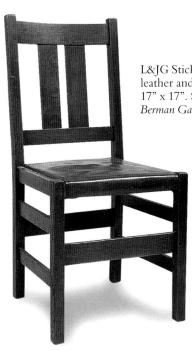

L&JG Stickley sidechair. Original leather and Handcraft mark. 36" x 17" x 17". $825. *Courtesy of the Berman Gallery, Philadelphia.*

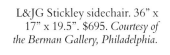

L&JG Stickley sidechair. 36" x 17" x 19.5". $695. *Courtesy of the Berman Gallery, Philadelphia.*

L&JG Stickley sidechair. 34.5" x 17" x 15.5. Set of four: $2,600. *Courtesy of Circa 1910 Antiques, Los Angeles.*

Stickley Brothers sidechair. 37" x 17.5" x 16". $750. *Courtesy of Circa 1910 Antiques, Los Angeles.*

Stickley Brothers chair, No. 42. 47" x 14.75" x 14". $950. *Courtesy of Circa 1910 Antiques, Los Angeles.*

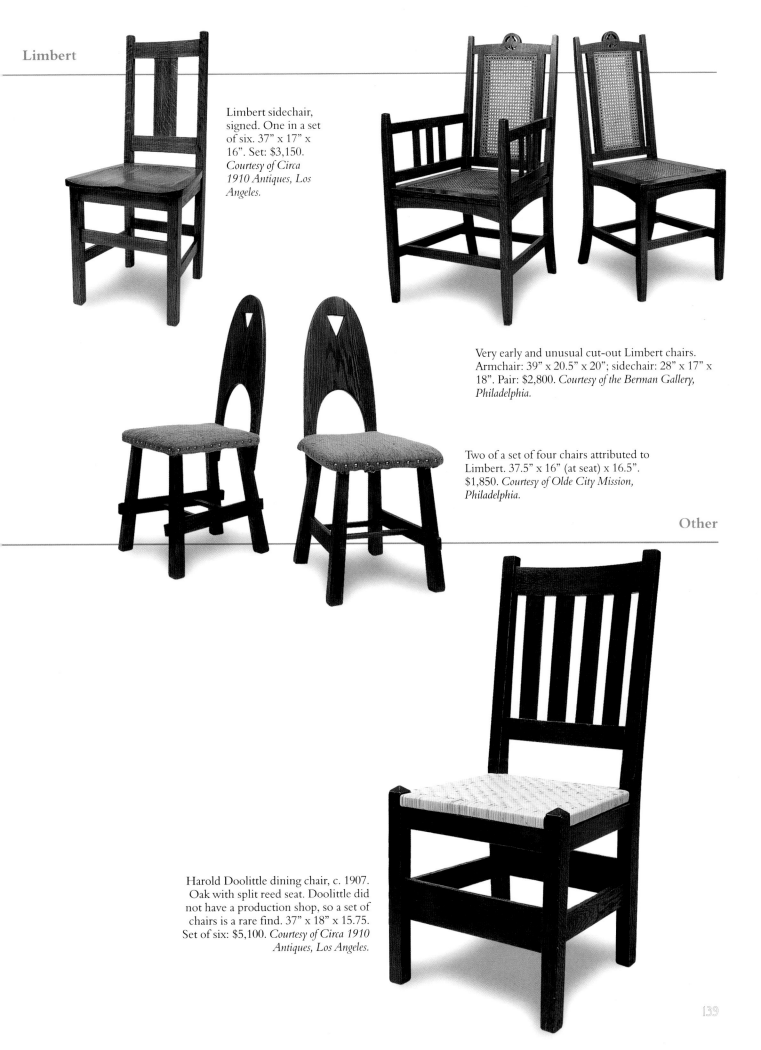

Limbert sidechair,
signed. One in a set
of six. 37" x 17" x
16". Set: $3,150.
*Courtesy of Circa
1910 Antiques, Los
Angeles.*

Very early and unusual cut-out Limbert chairs.
Armchair: 39" x 20.5" x 20"; sidechair: 28" x 17" x
18". Pair: $2,800. *Courtesy of the Berman Gallery,
Philadelphia.*

Two of a set of four chairs attributed to
Limbert. 37.5" x 16" (at seat) x 16.5".
$1,850. *Courtesy of Olde City Mission,
Philadelphia.*

Harold Doolittle dining chair, c. 1907.
Oak with split reed seat. Doolittle did
not have a production shop, so a set of
chairs is a rare find. 37" x 18" x 15.75.
Set of six: $5,100. *Courtesy of Circa 1910
Antiques, Los Angeles.*

Gustav Stickley

Gustav Stickley full-size bed with tapered posts. Original finish. Red decal and paper label. Headboard: 48" x 57.5". $6,500. *Courtesy of David Rago Auctions, Inc.*

Gustav Stickley spindled child's crib. Original finish. 34" x 55" x 35.5". $6,500-8,500. *Courtesy of David Rago Auctions, Inc.*

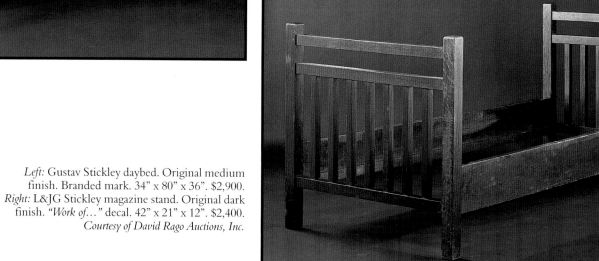

Left: Gustav Stickley daybed. Original medium finish. Branded mark. 34" x 80" x 36". $2,900. *Right:* L&JG Stickley magazine stand. Original dark finish. *"Work of…"* decal. 42" x 21" x 12". $2,400. *Courtesy of David Rago Auctions, Inc.*

Gustav Stickley, designs by Harvey Ellis. *Left:* Nine-drawer chest. Original condition. Red decal and paper label. 50.5" x 36" x 20". $16,000.
Right: Mirrored chest of drawers. Light overcoat on original finish, some minor veneer chips, but excellent condition. Red decal. 66" x 48" x 22". $3,750. *Courtesy of David Rago Auctions, Inc.*

Gustav Stickley mirrored dresser, no. 911. Original finish, branded in drawer. 65.5" x 48" x 22". $4,000. *Courtesy of Craftsman Auctions.*

Gustav Stickley slipper chair. 32.5" x 17" x 16". $2,400. *Courtesy of Circa 1910 Antiques, Los Angeles.*

L&JG Stickley five-drawer chest. $3,500.
Courtesy of Craftsman Auctions.

Stickley Brothers two-over-one-drawer night
stand. Original finish. $1,400. *Courtesy of
Craftsman Auctions.*

Limbert, tall chest. Refinished, branded mark. $2,700. *Courtesy of Craftsman Auctions.*

Roycroft mirrored six-drawer chest in its original ebonized finish. This may have been in the Roycroft Inn. Carved orb and cross mark. 52" tall (72" with the mirror) x 41" x 24". $7,500. *Courtesy of David Rago Auctions, Inc.*

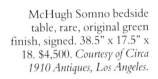

McHugh Somno bedside table, rare, original green finish, signed. 38.5" x 17.5" x 18. $4,500. *Courtesy of Circa 1910 Antiques, Los Angeles.*

McHugh signature on drawer bottom.

Chest. 66" x 42" x 21". $1,950.
*Courtesy of Olde City Mission,
Philadelphia.*

The lighting of the Arts & Crafts Movement coincided with the development of the electric light. While Edison invented the first successful electric incandescent light bulb in 1879, the prototype was far from practical, burning only 40 hours. Besides, there was no electric service available in homes. In 1907 the tungsten bulb was developed and by 1910 Edison was marketing his Mazda fixtures. It was not until 1913, however that it became economically practical for homes to convert from gas to electricity.

The changes are reflected in the lighting of the era. The Grueby Kendrick lamp seen in this chapter has work orders on the bottom for a conversion to electrification from its former life as a kerosene lamp. Several of the copper forms have evidence of being designed orginally for kerosene and being changed at some later date. Gradually, however, new forms were created that took advantage of the freedom electricity offered to the designer, and bulbous forms gave way to sleek and elegant new shapes.

Dirk Van Erp copper rivet lamp.
18" h. *Courtesy of Circa 1910
Antiques, Los Angeles.*

Dirk Van Erp/D'Arcy Gaw hammered copper lamp with mica
shade. *Courtesy of Circa 1910
Antiques, Los Angeles.*

Dirk Van Erp copper boudoir lamp. Original
patina, open box mark. $7,000. *Courtesy of
Craftsman Auctions.*

Dirk Van Erp, two-socket hammered copper table lamp, circa 1912. Closed-box signature. $15,000. *Courtesy of Craftsman Auctions.*

Dirk Van Erp/ D'Arcy Gaw hammered copper table lamp with mica and pierced copper shade. Original patina and mica, with some minor scratches and mottling. Open box and remnant of D'Arcy Gaw mark. 20" x 19" d. $22,500-27,500. *Courtesy of David Rago Auctions, Inc.*

Dirk Van Erp hammered copper and mica Warty table lam with unusual folded top. The three-panel mica shade cover three sockets. Some shade restoration and a new dark brown patina. Die stamped mark "San Francisco." 16" x 19.5". $25,000-35,000. *Courtesy of David Rago Auctions, Inc.*

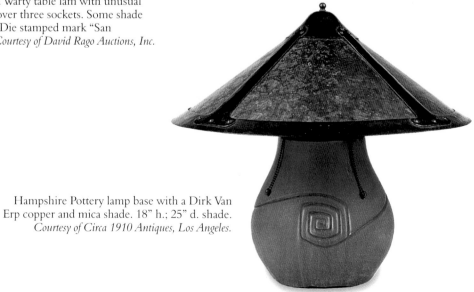

Hampshire Pottery lamp base with a Dirk Van Erp copper and mica shade. 18" h.; 25" d. shade. *Courtesy of Circa 1910 Antiques, Los Angeles.*

Gustav Stickley set of four hanging heart lanterns. These copper fixtures once hung in an original Craftsman Home in Braintree, Massachusetts. The glass is original. $8,500. *Courtesy of Craftsman Auctions.*

Gustav Stickley hammered copper table lamp, no. 609, with original patina. 21" x 14". $6,750. *Courtesy of Craftsman Auctions.*

Hammered copper base lamp by either Stickley Brothers or Limbert, with original silk and wicker shade. 18.5" h. $4,200. *Courtesy of Circa 1910 Antiques, Los Angeles.*

Heintz

Heintz Art Metal sterling silver and bronze lamp with pierced shade. 14" x 8". $4,800. *Courtesy of Circa 1910 Antiques, Los Angeles.*

Heintz lamp with mica shade. $2,250. *Courtesy of Craftsman Auctions.*

Handel trapezoidal desk lamp. Signed, original patina. $1,700. *Courtesy of Craftsman Auctions.*

Fulper lamp, 24" x 17". $1500. *Courtesy of Olde City Mission, Philadelphia.*

Fulper mushroom-shaped table lamp. Mirrored Black and Elephant's Breath Flambe glaze. The shade is made of free-form slag glass and red heart-shaped pieces. Short line in shade. Rectangular ink mark. 18" x 16" d. $11,000. *Courtesy of David Rago Auctions, Inc.*

Grueby Kendrick lamp base with a Tiffany Turtleback leaded glass shade. The base has seven handles with tooled leaves and a matte green glaze. This was originally an oil lamp, but was retooled at the Grueby factory to accommodate electricity. One label on the bottom records that it was originally sold with the turtleback shade and no shade was to be made. Another is the order for electrification. It also has a Grueby price tag ($125), a Grueby label and stamp. The shade and the font are stamped *Tiffany Studios/New York*. Vase: 12.5" x 10". Shade: 7" x 18" d. $260,000. *Courtesy of David Rago Auctions, Inc.*

Wheatley Pottery lamp base and leaded glass shade. 21" h; shade 16" d. *Courtesy of Circa 1910 Antiques, Los Angeles.*

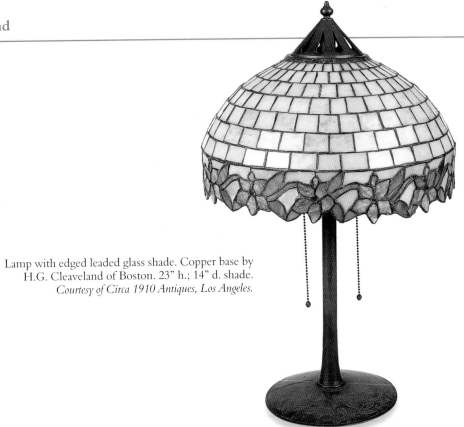

Lamp with edged leaded glass shade. Copper base by
H.G. Cleaveland of Boston. 23" h.; 14" d. shade.
Courtesy of Circa 1910 Antiques, Los Angeles.

Etched copper lamp with a pierced copper and mica
shade attributed to Forrest Craft Guild. 15" h. *Courtesy of
Circa 1910 Antiques, Los Angeles.*

Roycroft boudoir lamp designed by Dard Hunter with a leaded slag glass stage and a band of pink stylized blossoms. The base, which is old but not original to the shade, has its original patina, with replaced cap. Minor cracks in the glass. Impressed orb and cross mark. 14.75" x 7". $4,750. *Courtesy of David Rago Auctions, Inc.*

Two light bronze table lamp with slag glass and pierced bronze shade. *Courtesy of Olde City Mission, Philadelphia.*

Bronze table lamp with hexagonal stitched shade. *Courtesy of Olde City Mission, Philadelphia.*

Oak and metal table lamp with slag glass paneled shade. *Courtesy of Olde City Mission, Philadelphia.*

Bronze table lamp with eight panel slag glass and bronze shade. *Courtesy of Olde City Mission, Philadelphia.*

Lamp with cast bronze base and slag glass shade. 22" h. *Courtesy of Circa 1910 Antiques, Los Angeles.*

Chandelier with original patina. 15" x 20". $2,000. *Courtesy of Craftsman Auctions.*

Oak table lamp with reverse-painted slag glass and oak shade, no. L137. 21" x 14" x 14". $1,000. *Courtesy of Craftsman Auctions.*

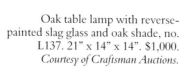

Though, in retrospect, the richly patinated copper of a Van Erp vase seems to epitomize the Arts & Crafts Movement, actually the medium of metal work came late to the creative mix. In England, C.R. Ashbee established metal work as one of the crafts in the Guild of Handicrafts, when he founded it in 1888. In America, most of the training and manufacturing of metal wares took place in large factories, such as Gorham Silver Company of Providence, Rhode Island.

That slowly changed as the new century approached. At Hull House, founded in Chicago in 1889 by Jane Addams and Ellen Gates Starr after a visit to Ashbee's guild and school, metal smithing was taught beginning in 1899. In the early years of the twentieth century formal classes began in the art schools. Pratt Institute and the Rhode Island School of Design both introduced metalworking programs in early 1901, followed by the Art Institute of Chicago and the Pennsylvania Museum School of Industrial Arts, both in 1903.

Two of the more productive sources of metal wares, Gustav Stickley and Roycroft, both entered the field from necessity. Stickley's work began with the heavy copper and brass hardware for his furniture. It was expanded to include a wide range of lighting fixtures, dishes, vases, plates and more, as well as iron work for fireplace equipment and architectural pieces. In the 1910 catalog, Stickley wrote,

...in the Craftsman scheme of interior decoration and furnishing
there is a well-defined place for the right kind of metal work. In fact, the

need for following out Craftsman designs in making all manner of household articles soon became as great as the original need for making furniture trim...[R]ooms finished with beams and wainscot in the Craftsman style needed the mellow glint of copper and brass here and there in lighting fixtures, lamps, and the like. As the glittering lacquered surfaces and more or less fantastic designs of machine-made fixtures were entirely out of harmony, we began to make lanterns of copper and brass after simple structural designs...and such articles as chafing dishes, trays, jardinières, umbrella stands and desk sets, our effort being all the time to keep articles within the bounds of the useful, letting their decorative value grow out of their fitness for that use and the quality of the design and workmanship.

In the case of Roycroft, metal work was produced by local craftsmen to provide hardware needed for the construction of the Roycroft buildings and the pulls and hinges needed for the furniture manufactured there. Strictly utilitarian, the designs of Roycroft metal wares did not blossom until the arrival of Karl Kipp in 1908.

On the West Coast, Dirk Van Erp settled in San Francisco in 1886 to work in the shipyards. In 1900 he began to create unique vessels from brass shell casings. The San Francisco galleries showed his work and by 1908 he had established his own studio.

By 1910, art metal had become an established craft with a broad patronage. The products of these artists continue to command respect and admiration from today's collectors.

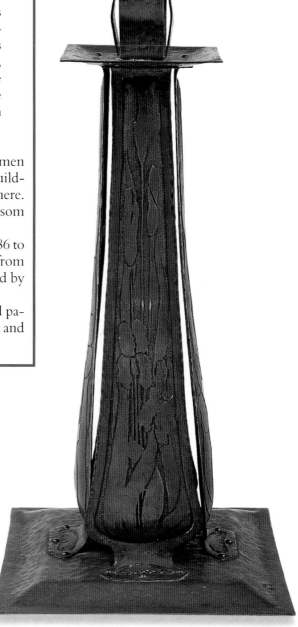

Dirk Van Erp
The Copper Shop
Oakland, California, 1908-1910
San Francisco, California, 1910-1977

Dirk Van Erp was born in Leeuwarden, the Netherlands in 1859, the oldest of seven children. His first exposure to metalwork was in the family hardware business. At 26 he left for America, settling in San Francisco, where he used his skills as a metalworker in the Navy shipyards on Mare Island.

At home his interests were more creative. In 1900 he began to produce art metal wares from brass shell casings. Art dealers in the San Francisco were impressed enough by his art to carry it in their shops.

Dirk Van Erp copper vase. 5", $950. *Courtesy of Olde City Mission, Philadelphia.*

In 1908 Van Erp opened the Copper Shop in Oakland, which had moved to San Francisco by 1910. In 1908 Harry Saint John Dixon, who later would open his own shop, apprenticed with Van Erp. Elizabeth Eleanor D'Arcy Gaw, a Canadian, worked in the San Francisco studio for a period of 11 months. Their names appear together on a windmill trademark that he adopted. Though of short duration, Gaw has been credited with bringing a new level of sophistication to Van Erp's work that continued for years. She returned to interior decorating in 1911.

Van Erp's work was all hand-wrought, the hammered surface being the only decorative feature. His "warty" textured vases are highly sought after, and especially with the red finish achieved by the annealing process.

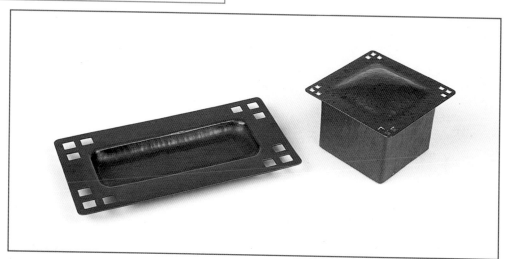

Dirk Van Erp copper inkwell and desk tray. Desk tray, 6.75" x 3.75". Inkwell, 2.5" h. Pair: $3,200. *Courtesy of Circa 1910 Antiques, Los Angeles.*

Van Erp mark on the bottom of the desk tray. *Courtesy of Circa 1910 Antiques, Los Angeles.*

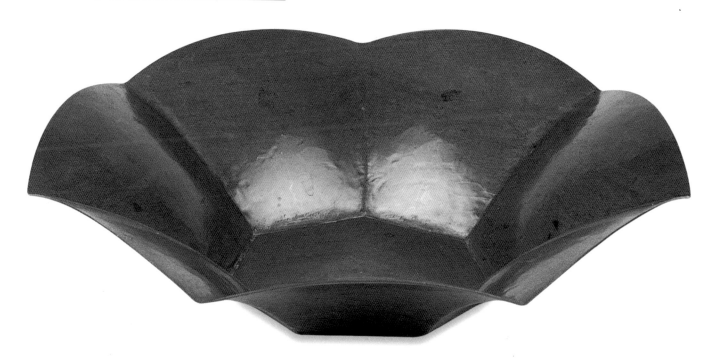

Dirk Van Erp septagonal copper bowl. 2.75" h. x 11" d. $1,850. *Courtesy of Circa 1910 Antiques, Los Angeles.*

Dirk Van Erp copper tray. 15.5" d.
$2,800. *Courtesy of Circa 1910
Antiques, Los Angeles.*

Dirk Van Erp copper vase
(drilled). 8.75" h. $2,800.
*Courtesy of Circa 1910 Antiques,
Los Angeles.*

Dirk Van Erp copper bowl. 1.5" h. x 6.25". $950. *Courtesy of Circa 1910 Antiques, Los Angeles.*

Dirk Van Erp copper bookends. 4.75" h. x 4.75" w. $1,450. *Courtesy of Circa 1910 Antiques, Los Angeles.*

Dirk Van Erp lobed copper bowl, seven segments. 3" h. x 9.75" d. $1,050. *Courtesy of Circa 1910 Antiques, Los Angeles.*

Dirk Van Erp Red Warty hammered copper bulbous pot. It has random hammering at the top and radial hammering at the bottom. Full-length dovetailed seam and original patina. 7.75" x 7". $14,000. *Courtesy of David Rago Auctions, Inc.*

Gustav Stickley

Gustav Stickley's venture into metalcraft grew from necessity: he needed hardware for his furniture. With his commitment to quality craft, he insisted upon the finest design, workmanship, and materials. Emphasizing lighting fixtures, Stickley also produced trays, candlesticks, desk sets, jardinieres, and more. Stickley never developed a distribution system as extensive as Roycroft's, so the work is much scarcer.

Gustav Stickley copper stamp box. 2.25" x 4" x 2". $925. *Courtesy of Circa 1910 Antiques, Los Angeles.*

Gustav Stickley hammered copper wares.
Back, left to right: Round tray with riveted handles. Original patina. Stamped *Craftsman* mark. 16" d. $2,000-3,000.
Large tray with embossed and cut-out rim pattern. Original patina, with normal wear marks. *Craftsman* stamp. 19.75" d. $2,000.
Rectangular tray with rolled edges. Original patina with normal wear marks. Impressed *Als Ik Kan* mark. 12" x 18.25". $1,700.
Front, left to right: Tall candlestick. Original patina with normal wear. Circular stamp mark. 12" x 6" x 6". $2,700.
Card tray with abstract repousse pattern. New patina. *Als Ik Kan* mark. 7.25" d. $325.
Chamberstick with riveted handle. Cleaned patina. *Als Ik Kan* mark. 8.75" x 6.75". $550. *Courtesy of David Rago Auctions, Inc.*

Gustav Stickley copper serving tray, no. 274. Enhanced patina. 16" diameter. $1,000. *Courtesy of Craftsman Auctions.*

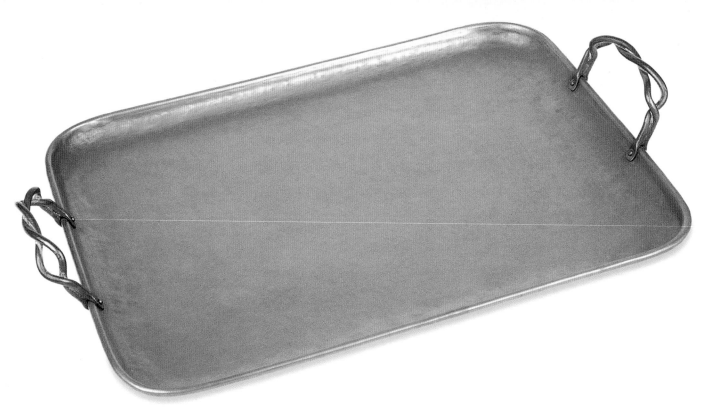

Gustav Stickley copper tray. 16" x 12". $2,500. *Courtesy of Circa 1910 Antiques, Los Angeles.*

Gustav Stickley hammered copper candlesticks. The left candle stick is earlier and more heavily hammered. Both 15" h. Left, $1,500; right $900. *Courtesy of Circa 1910 Antiques, Los Angeles.*

L&JG Stickley
Fayetteville, New York

L&JG Stickley most likely did not produce any metal wares, but their name appears on some pieces which were probably produced by Onandaga Shops and, later, Benedict Art Studios.

L&JG Stickley hammered copper tray. 17" d. $4,800. *Courtesy of Circa 1910 Antiques, Los Angeles.*

Onandaga Metal Shops, 1901-1904
(became Benedict Art Studio, 1904-?)
East Syracuse, New York

Produced copper wares of good quality, possibly supplying Gustav and L&JG Stickley.

Onondaga Metal Shops handled copper charger. 15" d. $1,250. *Courtesy of Circa 1910 Antiques, Los Angeles.*

Onandaga Metal Shops hammered copper planter. Original patina. 4.5" x 9.25". $500. *Courtesy of Craftsman Auctions.*

Stickley Brothers

Albert Stickley had opened a copper workshop near Grand Rapids by 1904. Like his brother, Gustav, his designs reflected the English crafts. Unlike Gustav or the Roycrofters, the origin of the copper shop was not utilitarian. According to Bruce Johnson (*The Official Price Guide to Arts and Crafts,* p. 372) he continued to outsource his furniture hardware to commercial firms. He employed Russian immigrant craftsmen to make decorative pieces such as lamps, trays, ewers, and vases.

Stickley Brothers copper vase. 9" h. $1,250. *Courtesy of Circa 1910 Antiques, Los Angeles.*

Stickley Brothers copper jardiniere. 7" h. x 11" d. $2,500. *Courtesy of Circa 1910 Antiques, Los Angeles.*

Roycroft

The beginnings of metalcraft at Roycroft were strictly utilitarian. At the turn of the century, the community that Elbert Hubbard was building needed hardware. To meet this need, Hubbard brought in local craftsmen to manufacture hinges, andirons, lighting, and hardware for the furniture. Having brought together a group of talented individuals, Hubbard, with his keen eye for business opportunities, began to offer their goods for sale. A rather thick and crudely fashioned copper tray and a letter opener appear in the 1906 furniture catalog, the first in a large line of copper items. Roycroft continued to turn out similar items until 1909 when Karl Kipp and Walter U. Jennings moved from the Roycroft book bindery to begin designing metal wares. Kipp was innately talented as a designer, and is generally credited with bringing a new creative energy to the copper shop. Jennings, formerly the manager of a knitting mill, who was drawn to Roycroft by Hubbard's writings, added organizational skills to the effort. Together they built the copper shop into a formidable enterprise with a broad list of creative products.

Both Kipp and Jennings left from 1911-1915 to start their own company, the Tookay Shop. They returned, however, in 1915, after Hubbard's death. In the years that followed, a national marketing strategy by Elbert Hubbard II distributed Roycroft to retailers in virtually every major community.

Roycroft metal work. *Back row, left to right:* American Beauty hammered copper vase. Minor dents and finish problems on original patina. Orb and cross mark. 18.5" x 7.5" d. $1,600.
Early hammered copper bulbous vase. Minor wear. Orb and cross mark. 5" x 4.5". $325.
Hammered copper cylindrical vase with verdigris band of stylized quatrefoils. Some minor wear. Orb and cross mark. 5" x 2.5" $350.
Pair of three-socket copper candelabra with a brass wash. Orb and cross mark. 20" x 9.5". $1,300.
Front row, left to right: Hammered copper Princess candlesticks. Original patina. Orb and cross mark 7.5" x 3.25". $650.
Hammered copper cabinet vase. Original patina. Orb and cross mark. 4.25" xc 2.25". $375.
Hammered copper covered bowl. Original dark patina. 2.5" x 6" x 375.
Footed nut bowl, hammered copper with three feet and rolled rim. Original patina. Orb and cross mark. 4" x 10". $900.
Roycroft ceramic salt and pepper shakers, designed by Dard Hunter and made by Buffalo Pottery. Small chip on bottom of salt shaker. 3" x 2". $375.
Hammered copper dinner bell. Original patina. 3" x 1.75". $450. *Courtesy of David Rago Auctions, Inc.*

Roycroft accessories. *Back row, left to right:* Hammered copper bookends, decorated with heavily relieved tree. Original patina. Early orb and cross mark. 6.5" x 4". $7,500.
Hammered copper vase with reticulated German silver design. Original patina. Orb and cross mark. 6.25" x 3". $1,800.
Hammered copper cylindrical vase with tooled polychrome floral design. Original patina with minor wear. Early orb and cross mark. 7" x 2.5". $1,800.
Front row, left to right: Hammered copper vase in original medium-dark patina. Orb and cross mark. 4.25" x 6.5". $800.
Oak letter box with original finish. Carved orb and cross mark. 3.25" x 10" x 13". $1,200.
Hammered copper dish with tooled ivy leaves. Original patina. Early orb and cross mark. 5.75" d. $475.
Tooled leather woman's purse. Minor wear to strap. Orb and cross mark. $600. *Courtesy of David Rago Auctions, Inc.*

Roycroft American Beauty copper vase. 12.5", $1,650. *Courtesy of Olde City Mission, Philadelphia.*

Roycroft copper vase. 4.5" tall. $295. *Courtesy of Olde City Mission, Philadelphia.*

Roycroft copper candlesticks. 13", $1,350 pair. *Courtesy of Olde City Mission, Philadelphia.*

Roycroft Princess copper candlesticks. Original patina, signed with impressed orb. $850. *Courtesy of Craftsman Auctions.*

Roycroft hammered copper and ceramic chafing dish. The ceramic dish is by Redwing. 10" h; 14" d. tray. $2,500. *Courtesy of Circa 1910 Antiques, Los Angeles.*

Karl Kipp

Karl Kipp came to Roycroft in 1908, leaving his job as a banker and moving his family in search of a new beginning. Starting in the bindery, he displayed a talent for design that caught Hubbard's eye. He tapped him to take the fledgling Copper Shop, which had focused primarily on fashioning hardware for the furniture, and turn it into a flourishing, creative entity. By 1909 the Copper Shop was staffed with talented craftsmen who produced a line of metal ware extensive enough and beautiful enough to warrant its own catalog.

In 1911, after three years of success, Kipp and Walter U. Jennings left Roycroft to form the Tookay Shop, also in East Aurora, New York. For four years they produced copper, pewter, and silver wares in a continuation of their Roycroft style. All evidence is that their endeavor was successful. However, after the elder Hubbard's death in 1915, they were asked to return to Roycroft by Elbert Hubbard II. They did so, and Roycroft undertook a national sales campaign for their metal wares that made them a popular commodity until the stock market crash of 1929. Kipp continued at Roycroft until 1931.

Karl Kipp Roycroft copper planter. 3.5" x 7.5", $1,800. *Courtesy of Olde City Mission, Philadelphia.*

Art Crafts Shop

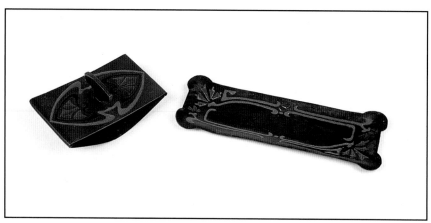

The Art Crafts Shop pen tray and blotter, enameled bronze. $475. *Courtesy of Circa 1910 Antiques, Los Angeles.*

Mark of the Art Crafts Shop. *Courtesy of Circa 1910 Antiques, Los Angeles.*

Chambersticks from the Art Crafts Shop. Enameled copper in original patina. 7.5" tall. $600. *Courtesy of Craftsman Auctions.*

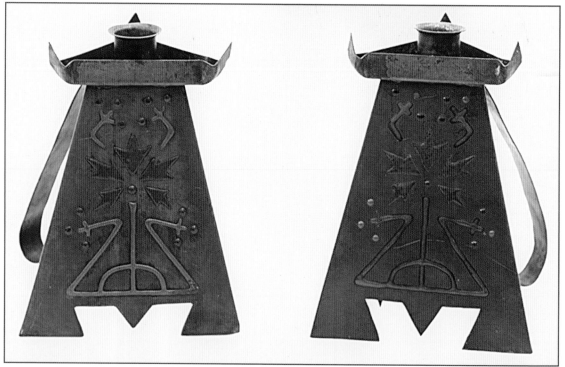

Heintz Art Metal, bronze vase with silver inlay. 7.5" h. $1,250. *Courtesy of Circa 1910 Antiques, Los Angeles.*

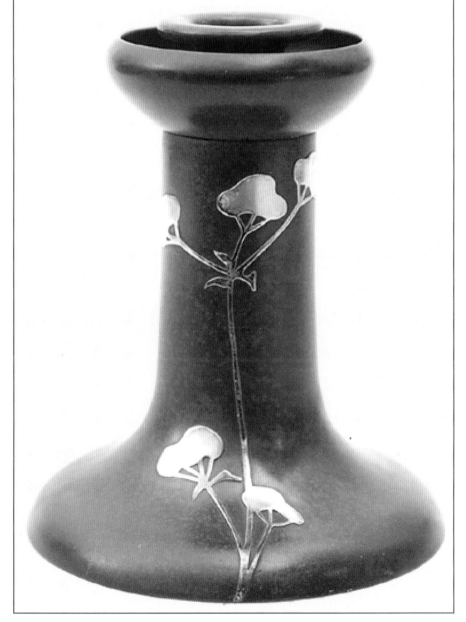

Heintz candlestick. Original patina, signed. 5.25" tall. $350-450. *Courtesy of Craftsman Auctions.*

Left: Heintz vase. Original finish, signed. 4.25" tall. $375. *Courtesy of Craftsman Auctions.*

Right: Heintz vase, signed. 11.25" tall. $400. *Courtesy of Craftsman Auctions.*

Silvercrest five-piece desk set. *Courtesy of Circa 1910 Antiques, Los Angeles.*

Harry Saint John Dixon
San Francisco, 1908-1967

Born in 1890, Dixon studied with Van Erp in 1908. For several years he worked for various metal shops before opening his own in 1920. He used natural design motifs, marking them with a stamp of a man forging a bowl.

Harry Dixon vase, hammered brass. 7.5" h. $1,650. *Courtesy of Circa 1910 Antiques, Los Angeles.*

Harry Dixon mark. *Courtesy of Circa 1910 Antiques, Los Angeles.*

Old Mission Kopper Kraft
Jauchen's Ye Olde Copper Shop
Brosi's Ye Olde Copper Shoppe
San Jose and San Francisco, California, c. 1922-1925

Hans W. Jauchen, born in Germany, and Fred T. Brosi, an Italian native, worked together in the Old Mission Kopper Kraft from about 1922 to 1925. Old Mission manufacturing was located in San Jose, with the retail outlet in San Francisco. Before and after, they were involved in a number of other metalsmith businesses, including the two similarly named companies represented here. Brosi died in 1935, Jauchen in 1970.

Old Mission Kopperkraft, two carved trays. 4.75" d. $275 each.
Courtesy of Circa 1910 Antiques, Los Angeles.

Mark of Old Mission Kopperkraft.

Fred Brosi's Ye Olde Copper Shoppe San Francisco bowl. 6.25" d. x 2.25" h. *Courtesy of Circa 1910 Antiques, Los Angeles.*

Bradley & Hubbard
Meriden, Connecticut. 1854-early 20th century

Based in Meriden, Connecticut, Bradley & Hubbard created a variety of cast bronze decorative items, including lamps with slag glass shades, desk wares, candlesticks and more.

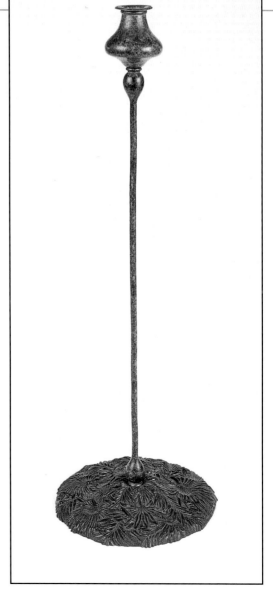

Bradley & Hubbard candlestick. 23", $695. *Courtesy of Olde City Mission, Philadelphia.*

Jarvie candlesticks. Left: Alpha, 11" h. $950. Middle: Delta, 14" h., $2,200. Right: name unknown, 24" h. *Courtesy of Circa 1910 Antiques, Los Angeles.*

WMF (Wurttemburgische Mettalwaren Fabrik)
Geislingen, Germany
Still in operation today, WMF manufactured metalwares by well-known German artists, many of which were exported to Liberty & Co. and other English firms. They produced an English catalog and their designs at the turn of the century reflect the Arts & Crafts and Art Nouveau influences.

WNF Austrian hammered copper, brass and bamboo tea pot and warmer. 13.25" h. $650. *Courtesy of Circa 1910 Antiques, Los Angeles.*

Frost Arts & Crafts Workshop
Dayton, Ohio, c. 1915

Founded by George W. Frost, this company produced copper and brass goods in the early 1900s. It was located in Dayton, Ohio.

Etched brass picture frame. Frost Co., Dayton, Ohio. 8", $695. *Courtesy of Olde City Mission, Philadelphia.*

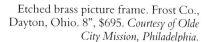

The Mission Inn,
Riverside, California

The historic Mission Inn began, in 1876, as The Glenwood. It was built by Christopher Columbus Miller. His eldest son, Frank, purchased the Inn from his father for $5000 in 1880, and began his career as the "Master of the Inn." In 1902, he built a Mission Revival style building, based on a design by Arthur B. Benton. To outfit his new inn, Miller purchased especially designed furniture (made by Limbert) and accessories, including the copper wine cooler shown here. They all bear the mission bell logo.

Mission Inn three-handled wine cooler, logo on front. 7" h. $475. *Courtesy of Circa 1910 Antiques, Los Angeles.*

185

Copper bookends. 9", $295; 5", $550; 5", $495. *Courtesy of Olde City Mission, Philadelphia.*

Small hammered brass bowl. 5" d. x 1" h. *Courtesy of Circa 1910 Antiques, Los Angeles.*

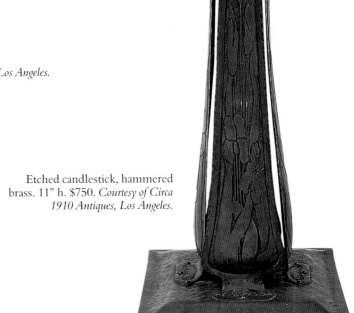

Etched candlestick, hammered brass. 11" h. $750. *Courtesy of Circa 1910 Antiques, Los Angeles.*

Two-slot copper letter holder. 5" x 8" x 2.5". $1,150. *Courtesy of Circa 1910 Antiques, Los Angeles.*

Strong box. Hammered copper. 2.5" x 8.5" x 6.5", $350. *Courtesy of Olde City Mission, Philadelphia.*

The growth of art pottery at the end of the nineteenth century is one of the most highly valued expressions of the Arts & Crafts Movement. Ironically it was also one of its most purely "artistic" expressions. Until this time the pottery made in America was strictly utilitarian: stoneware crocks, bottles, candleholders, tableware; redware dishes, cups, baking ware; yellow ware mixing bowls and pitchers. While many of the pieces were intrinsically beautiful, often showing the creative flair of their makers, they were meant for everyday use in the kitchen or dining room. In a sense this early American pottery was the precursor of the Arts & Crafts pottery.

This is not to say that there was not an ample supply of artistic pottery in America. Prior to 1870, imports from England, Germany, France, and Asia could be found in nearly every respectable home. Their purpose was more decorative than utilitarian, and often they expressed the same sort of gaudiness that was evidenced in Victorian-style furniture.

But soon an indigenous American art pottery movement developed: Alexander and Hugh Robertson, Chelsea Keramic Studio, Boston, 1872; Mary Louise McLaughlin, Losanti, Cincinnati, 1877; Mary Longworth Nichols, Rookwood, Cincinnati, 1880; George Ohr, Beloxi, Mississippi, 1880; T.J. Wheatley, Cincinnati, 1880; Alexander Robertson and Linna Irelan, Roblin Art Pottery, San Francisco, 1884; William Gates, Terra Cotta, Illinois, 1886; Theolphilus Brouwer, Long Island, New York, 1894; William Grueby, Boston, 1894. These and many more potters began experimenting with clays, glazes, and forms to create a pottery that would be truly an artistic expression of their own creativity.

By the end of the nineteenth century it became clear to many art educators that there was a need for an American art pottery. Schools be-

gan adding pottery programs to their curricula. Charles Binns came to New Jersey from England to direct the pottery program at the Trenton Technical School of Science and Art and supervise the operations of its sponsor, the Ceramic Art Company, later to become Lenox China. When Alfred University began the New York School of Clayworking and Ceramics in 1900, they called Binns as its first director. From that position he would have a far reaching influence on a generation of potters, enhanced even more by his seminal writings in the field. Other schools followed suit, including Newcomb College in New Orleans, the Art Institute of Chicago, The Pratt Institute, and the Pennsylvania Museum School of Industrial Art among others.

In 1904 Dr. Herbert Hall opened a sanatorium in Marblehead, Massachusetts for those suffering from mental illness. As one of the therapies, which he also hoped would help finance the hospital, he opened a pottery, led by Arthur Baggs, a student of Charles Binns. Other health and social institutions followed suit: Arequipa Pottery in Northern California, initially directed by Frederick Rhead; Halycon Pottery headed by Alexander Robertson, and part of a utopian community in Pismo Beach, California; The Saturday Evening Girls, of Boston, directed by Thomas Nickerson.

Many more small potteries would be born in the early years of the twentieth century, most with direct connections back to these earlier potteries. These include Ernest Batchelder of Batchelder Tile, William V. Bragdon and Chauncey R. Thomas of California Faience, Artus Van Briggle, and Abraham Fulper of Fulper Pottery. They and many others helped establish a tradition in American art pottery that continues to this day.

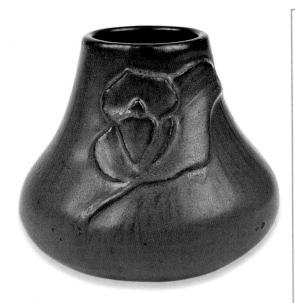

Arequipa small vase. 3.5" h. $2,200. *Courtesy of Circa 1910 Antiques, Los Angeles.*

Arequipa, Fairfax, California

Dr. Philip King Brown began the Arequipa Tuberculosis Sanitorium at Fairfax, California, in 1911, as a nursing facility for young women. To help patients pass the long hours of recuperative time creatively, he began programs of therapy that included basket weaving, loom weaving, typing, and other activities, none of which proved entirely satisfactory. Learning of the programs at Marblehead (Marblehead Pottery) and in the North End of Boston (the Saturday Evening Girls), Brown decided that a pottery might provide the outlet he sought and would produce income for the continuance of the Sanatorium.

Brown brought Frederick H. Rhead to help organize the program. Rhead had been trained as a potter by his father in England before coming to work in a number of American potteries, including Avon, Weller, Roseville, and Jervis. He set up the pottery and trained the young women to do every task that their strength allowed. It was good therapy, but not profitable. Rhead left in 1914, and was replaced by Albert L. Solon, who moved the pottery closer to success. He was followed by F.H. Wilde, who reorganized the pottery and put it on a better footing. Just when success seemed at hand, World War I placed its demands on the economy and the pottery closed its doors in 1918. The Sanitorium continued in operation until 1957.

Most Arequipa pottery was made from local clays. Pieces were thrown, pressed, or cast. Some were glazed and some had incised or raised designs. Pieces had a thick, sturdy look.

Bauer Pottery
Paducah, Kentucky and Los Angeles, California, 1885-1962

J.A. Bauer Pottery Company had its roots in Paducah, Kentucky, where it was started by John Andrew Bauer in 1885. In 1910 he moved the operation, molds and all to the Lincoln Heights area of Los Angeles, California. The company closed in 1962.

Bauer vase. 8" x 7". *Courtesy of Circa 1910 Antiques, Los Angeles.*

Hand-painted Bavarian bowl, c. 1900.
5.5" h. x 9" d. $525. *Courtesy of Circa 1910
Antiques, Los Angeles.*

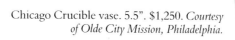

Chicago Crucible vase. 5.5". $1,250. *Courtesy
of Olde City Mission, Philadelphia.*

Clewell Metal Art
Canton, Ohio, c. 1906-1965

Charles W. Clewell founded his business in Canton, Ohio, in 1906, not so much to pot as to decorate pottery by adhering a thin coating of metal on a ceramic base. The ceramics were purchased from other Ohio potteries. He perfected his technique over the years yielding a realistic surface effect and patina. The company closed in 1965.

Clewell drink set, pitcher and six cups,
on Gustav Stickley tray. Set without the
tray: $1,600. *Courtesy of Circa 1910
Antiques, Los Angeles.*

Arthur Cole (attributed), Southern pottery. 13", $350. *Courtesy of Olde City Mission, Philadelphia.*

Fulper Pottery
Flemington, New Jersey, 1910-1935

Abraham Fulper bought Samuel Hill's drain tile pottery in 1860. Fulper continued Hill's basic line before diversifying into earthenware and stoneware. When the senior Fulper died in 1881, his sons, George W., William H., and Edward B. continued the pottery. At first, Fulper made only drain tiles, but soon produced earthenware and stoneware. Vinegar jugs, pickling jars, bottles, beer mugs, butter churns, bowls, and "drinking fountains for poultry" were also produced at the pottery.

The firm was under the direction of William H. Fulper II, Abraham's grandson, by the early 1900s. Martin Stangl became Fulper's ceramics engineer in 1911, and helped invent a group of famille rose glazes, including ashes of roses, deep rose, peach bloom, old rose, and true rose. Stangl left in 1914 or 1915 to work for Haeger in Dundee, Illinois. The

Fulper vases. 9", $750; 5", $325; 8", $395. *Courtesy of Olde City Mission, Philadelphia.*

Fulper Pottery won several awards at the 1915 San Francisco Panama Pacific International Exposition.

The Vasekraft line was produced using classical and oriental shapes. The firm made lamps (after 1910), pottery lampshades (often set with glass), ashtrays, cigarette boxes, vases, bowls, and other giftwares. The firm also made the "Fulper Germ Proof Filter," a set of jars that held cold drinking water. They even made dolls' heads for a short time. In 1920, the firm introduced the first solid-colored glazed dinnerware produced in the United States; green was the only color used for the dinnerwares until 1930, when other colors were added.

The Fulper Pottery continued to expand, and in 1926 acquired the Anchor Pottery Company of Trenton, New Jersey. A fire in 1929 destroyed the Fulper buildings in Flemington, and the firm decided to move most of its operations to the Trenton plant. Artware was still made on a small scale in Flemington until 1935.

Fulper candlestick. 6". $195. *Courtesy of Olde City Mission, Philadelphia.*

Fulper bowl. 5" h. $850. *Courtesy of Circa 1910 Antiques, Los Angeles.*

Fulper vase. 17.5" h. $3800. *Courtesy of Circa 1910 Antiques, Los Angeles.*

Fulper vase. 13.25" h. $1,250. *Courtesy of Circa 1910 Antiques, Los Angeles.*

Grueby Faience Company
Boston, Massachusetts, 1894-1911

William Grueby founded the Grueby Pottery in 1894 at the age of 27. He had received his training at the J. and J.G. Low Art Tile Works in Chelsea. After ten years he left Low to form his own business focusing on architectural terra cotta and decorative tiles. In 1897 the Grueby Faience Company was incorporated, bringing on board the design expertise of George Prentiss Kendrick, who along with William H. Graves was a partner in the new entity. With Kendrick's designs, known for their rich organic forms, and the innovative matte glazes, the genius of Grueby art pottery was recognized almost at once. Many pieces went directly from the studio to the museums. Others found their way into Tiffany lamp bases or as tiles in Gustav Stickley furniture. Grueby closed his art pottery operations in 1911, and ended operations completely upon its sale to C. Pardee Works of Perth Amboy, New Jersey in 1919.

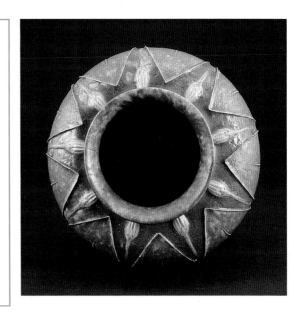

Grueby floor vase by Wilhemina Post. A beautiful, large form in excellent condition. Circular pottery mark, incised *WP*. 15.5" x 10". $60,000. *Courtesy of David Rago Auctions, Inc.*

Grueby pottery (has rim chip). 3" h. x 4.25" d. $750.
Courtesy of Circa 1910 Antiques, Los Angeles.

Grueby vase. 8" h. x 3.5" d. $1, 200.
Courtesy of Circa 1910 Antiques, Los Angeles.

Grueby vase. 8.5". *Courtesy of Olde City Mission, Philadelphia.*

Grueby ship tile. 6" x 6". $1,250. *Courtesy of Craftsman Auctions.*

Grueby floor vase. This is one of only two known in this form and represents one of the largest of the two-tone vases. Minor glaze chips to the base and nicks to edges of the leaves. Factory label. 23.25" x 8.5". $25,000. *Courtesy of David Rago Auctions, Inc.*

Grueby vases. *Left:* Gourd-shaped vase designed by G.P. Kendrick. Small glaze chips and minor restoration. Stamped circular pottery mark/artist's cipher. 12" x 8.25". $20,000.
Right: Floor vase of exceptional height. Some restoration and minor chips. Circular and rectangular paper labels. 21" x 8". $21,000. *Courtesy of David Rago Auctions, Inc.*

Hampshire Pottery
Keene, New Hampshire, 1871-1916

Founded in Keene, New Hampshire, by James S. Taft, Hampshire Pottery began producing in 1871. A successful venture, they hired Thomas Stanley in 1879 to oversee expansion in two new plants. They produced majolica and transfer ware. In 1883 they introduced a matt glaze that would adorn a popular line of art pottery. The pottery was sold to George M. Morton in 1916 and closed its doors in 1916.

Hampshire vase. 10", $1,050. *Courtesy of Olde City Mission, Philadelphia.*

Marblehead Pottery
Marblehead, Massachusetts, 1904-1936

Marblehead Pottery was founded in 1904 by Dr. Herbert J. Hall, as one of several therapeutic activities for his patients in his Marblehead, Massachusetts sanatorium. He brought in Arthur Baggs to run the operations. This 19-year-old man from Alfred University, New York, was recommended by Charles Binns, the first director of the New York School of Clayworking and Ceramics at Alfred University. Under Baggs's direction the Marblehead Pottery grew until, by 1908, its production reached 200 pieces per day. It had, in fact,

Marblehead vase. 5", $3,500. *Courtesy of Olde City Mission, Philadelphia.*

Marblehead Pottery vases. 4"; 9"; 4".
Courtesy of Olde City Mission, Philadelphia.

outgrown its original purpose of providing therapy, and professional artisans were brought in to augment the patient workers. By 1915 the pottery had grown to such a size that it became disassociated from the sanatorium and came under the sole ownership of Baggs. Though its professional staff was more productive, the pottery remained small, making hand-thrown and glazed pots throughout its existence. Only six people worked at the factory in 1916. Its doors were closed in 1936. Baggs taught at Ohio State University from 1928 until his death in 1947.

Marblehead Pottery vases. 4", $850; 6", $1,250; chamberstick, 8", $750. *Courtesy of Olde City Mission, Philadelphia.*

Marblehead Pottery. *Left to right:* Bulbous vase incised with stylized tree pattern. 1" hairline to rim. Impressed ship mark and MT. 6.25" x 3.75". $3,250.
Large bulbous vase decorated with flying geese. Typical minor glaze bubbles. Impressed ship mark and MP. 9" x 7". $10,000-15,000.
Ovoid vase by Hannah Tutt embossed with fruit and leaf pattern. Impressed ship mark and HT. 5" x 3.75". $1,300. *Courtesy of David Rago Auctions, Inc.*

Marblehead Pottery. *Back row, left to right:* Tall chamberstick with rounded handle, rare. Impressed ship mark. 8.5" x 5". $500.
Tall vase. Stamped MP ship mark, remnant of paper label. 8" x 4.25". $1000.
Straight-sided vase impressed with stylized flowers and leaves. Ship mark and M. 4" x 3.25". $1,800. *Front row, left to right:* Squat bulbous vase. Impressed mark. 3.25" x 5". $450.
Flared bowl with embossed lotus pattern. Stilt-pull chips. Stamped ship mark. 3.75" x 8". $325.
Pair of bookends, each embossed with different ship. Some running of glaze and minor restoration. Each bears ship stamp. 5.5" x 5.5". $800. *Courtesy of David Rago Auctions, Inc.*

Newcomb College Pottery
New Orleans, Louisiana, 1895-1939

Newcomb College Pottery was developed as part of the educational program at Sophia Newcomb Memorial College for Women, in New Orleans, in 1895. The brainchild of Ellsworth Woodward, the pottery was an attempt to introduce practical, marketable art education so that the students would be able to find productive, meaningful work after graduation. Mary G. Sheerer, an experienced ceramicist familiar with Rookwood Pottery, was hired as co-director, and she made Newcomb Pottery her life's work. Joseph Fortune Meyer was hired to run the clay shop. He would throw all the pots to Sheerer's specifications. The young women would then add the decoration. The pottery closed in 1939, though the Newcomb Guild continued to use the pottery mark until 1948.

Newcomb Pottery. *Left:* early carved vase by Marie Ross, 1903. Small chip to rim. Stamped *NC/MROSS?JM/X33*. 5.5" x 5". $12,000. *Right:* Early milk pitcher by Mazie Ryan, 1904. Two small glazed-over firing lines. In ink: NC/YY38/M.T.RYAN/JM. 8" x 5.5". $8,500. *Courtesy of David Rago Auctions, Inc.*

Eagle Pottery
Niloak Pottery
Benton, Arkansas, 1910-1946

Charles Hyten and his two brothers inherited the Eagle Pottery from their father. Located in Benton, Arkansas it produced mainly commercial stoneware. Charles Hyten developed the signature swirled colors using mixtures of local clay, producing the first successful pieces in 1910 after much experimentation. The pottery was renamed Niloak in 1911 and continued in operation until 1946.

Niloak vases. 5.5", $550; 5.5", $175. *Courtesy of Olde City Mission, Philadelphia.*

Niloak pottery vases. 3" to 8.25". *Courtesy of Circa 1910 Antiques, Los Angeles.*

199

George Ohr
Biloxi, Mississippi, 1885-1907

George Ohr produced pottery at his studio in Biloxi, Mississippi from 1885 to 1907. Producing nearly 10,000 pieces, he sold almost none, and the collection remaining largely together until discovered in an attic by Jim Carpenter in 1972. Ohr died in 1918, decades before his work found the respect and market it had failed to find during his life.

George Ohr small vase. 3.5" h. x 1.25" d. $1,400. *Courtesy of Circa 1910 Antiques, Los Angeles.*

Paul Revere Pottery and Saturday Evening Girls
Boston and Brighton, Massachusetts, 1906-1942

In 1906 a group of Boston philanthropists, seeking to improve the lot of underprivileged young women, established The Paul Revere Pottery. Edith Brown a librarian in the North End of Boston, was the first director. At the beginning the girls gathered in the basement of an old house, and were known as the "Saturday Evening Girls." Mrs. James R. Storrow, one of the original benefactors, bought a building near Old North Church for the group, equipped with a large kiln and all the supplies that were necessary. The Saturday Evening Girls grew to about 200 young women.

The pottery that they produced had an international market, but it never produced a sustaining level of profit. Continued support through Mrs. Storrow and others allowed it to remain in operation, though in 1915 the size was reduced as it moved to Brighton. In 1942 the pottery closed.

Paul Revere Pottery vases. Yellow: Saturday Evening Girls (SEG): 7" h., $2,000. Green: 10" h., $1,600. *Courtesy of Circa 1910 Antiques, Los Angeles.*

Peters and Reed Pottery Company
Zane Pottery Company
South Zanesville, Ohio, 1898-1901

Founded by John D. Peters and Adam Reed, the Peters and Reed Pottery Company began in 1898 in South Zanesville, Ohio. In 1921 its name was changed to the Zane Pottery Company. Their art pottery line took form in 1901.

Peters & Reed vase. 7.5", $475.
Courtesy of Olde City Mission, Philadelphia.

Peters & Reed. Vases: 3.5", $375; 11.5", $350.
Courtesy of Olde City Mission, Philadelphia.

Pisgah Forest Pottery
Pisgah, North Carolina, 1926-present

Founded by Walter Benjamin Stephen in Pisgah Forest, North Carolina, in 1926. It is known for dark glazed pots with cameo-like decorations. (Rago, p. 254). Stephen died in 1961, but the pottery continues.

Pisgah vase, forest green. 7" h. $275. *Courtesy of Circa 1910 Antiques, Los Angeles.*

Rookwood Pottery
Cincinnati, Ohio

Maria Longworth Nichols (Storer) was born in Cincinnati, Ohio, into one of the richest and most prestigious families in the region. In her twenties she studied china painting with Maria Eggers at the University of Cincinnati School of Design, of which her first husband, George Ward Nichols, was one of the founders. Having exhibited at the Centennial in Philadelphia, Nichols attended the exhibit. She was taken with the French and Japanese exhibits, and returned to Cincinnati inspired to experiment with different clays and glazes, including underglaze slip decoration. She and M. Louise McLaughlin set up studios at the Frederick Dallas Pottery, but found the kilns too hot for their delicately rendered decoration.

Her father purchased an abandoned schoolhouse, which Nichols converted into a studio, and on Thanksgiving day, 1880 Rookwood Pottery was born, named after the family homestead. Rookwood was Ohio's first art pottery. Its first full-time decorator was Albert M. Valentien, who with his wife Anna Marie, also a Rookwood artist, later established the Valentien Pottery in San Diego, California.

Rookwood vase, 4", $1,095. *Courtesy of Olde City Mission, Philadelphia.*

Artist decorated Rookwood vases. Left to right: 8", Vera Tischler, $950; 6", William Henschel, $1,250; 8", Charles Todd, $2,300. *Courtesy of Olde City Mission, Philadelphia.*

Despite its creativity, the pottery depended upon the Longworth family largesse for its early survival. In 1883, William Taylor took over the management of the pottery, and over the next five years moved it toward profitability. In 1890 he took over ownership of Rookwood, as Maria remarried after her first husband's death and lost interest in the business.

Taylor encouraged the talented artists of Rookwood, including Laura Fry, Artus Van Briggle, Katara Shiragyamadani, the Valentiens, William McDonald, and Matt Daly. New glazes were developed as were new techniques for underglaze slip decoration.

In 1889, the pottery was internationally recognized with a gold medal at the Exposition Universelle in Paris, first prize gold metal at the Exhibition of American Art Industry in Philadelphia, and numerous other honors over the following decade.

Taylor died unexpectedly in 1913. As the demand for hand decorated art pottery dried up after 1920, the company found a market for molded pottery, keeping it going until the pressures of the Depression forced the layoffs of most of the decorators. The company limped along, declaring bankruptcy in 1941. After changing hands several times, Rookwood's production finally ceased in 1967.

Rookwood 6.5" $495. Charles Todd. *Courtesy of Olde City Mission, Philadelphia.*

Rookwood, 1910, signed by Henschel. 3.5" h. $1,650. *Courtesy of Circa 1910 Antiques, Los Angeles.*

Dragonfly vases. Left and center: Rookwood, 8"
$1,150; 9", 1050. Right: Van Briggle: 7", $495.
Courtesy of Olde City Mission, Philadelphia.

Rookwood vases. Left: Greek key design, 8"
$900, right: a pair of five-sided vases. 5", $425
each. *Courtesy of Olde City Mission, Philadelphia.*

Rookwood vases. 7" $575; 7", $650; 6", $350.
Courtesy of Olde City Mission, Philadelphia.

Rookwood candlesticks. 8", $1,575 pair. *Courtesy of Olde City Mission, Philadelphia.*

Rookwood, Fred Rothenbush scenic vase, 1920. $1,200. *Courtesy of Craftsman Auctions.*

Rookwood, Lenore Asbury scenic vase, 1927. $1,800-2,500. *Courtesy of Craftsman Auctions.*

Rookwood vase by Carl Schmidt, signed. It has a factory "x" for glaze imperfections. 10" tall. $2,000. *Courtesy of Craftsman Auctions.*

Roseville Carnelian vases, 1910-1915. Left to right: 7", $395; 7", $325; 7", $375. *Courtesy of Olde City Mission, Philadelphia.*

Roseville Falline vase, 1933. 6.5", $1,300. *Courtesy of Olde City Mission, Philadelphia.*

Roseville Dogwood vase, 1916-1919. 7.5", $275. *Courtesy of Olde City Mission, Philadelphia.*

Roseville Jonquil, 1931. 12.5", $1,250.
Courtesy of Olde City Mission, Philadelphia.

Roseville bowl. 9" d. *Courtesy of Circa 1910 Antiques, Los Angeles.*

Roseville Pinecone console bowl. $1,095. *Courtesy of Olde City Mission, Philadelphia.*

Roseville basket. 10.5",
$425. *Courtesy of Olde City
Mission, Philadelphia.*

Large Roseville Mostique
vase, $750. *Courtesy of Olde
City Mission, Philadelphia.*

Roycroft
East Aurora, New York

Pottery at Roycroft was not the large scale operation that furniture and metalwork were. Both Jerome Conner and Dard Hunter did some work in this area, but examples are very rare. Somewhat more plentiful are table pieces made for Roycroft by Buffalo Pottery.

Buffalo Pottery, Roycroft sugar bowl with lid.
Signed. Tight line crack and small chips. $550.
Courtesy of Craftsman Auctions.

Teco Ware (Gates Potteries)
Terra Cotta, Illinois, 1901-early 1920s

William Day Gates was a Chicago attorney when he began the American Terra Cotta and Ceramic Company in 1886. Specializing in architectural tiles and decorative bricks, it was to be the firm foundation of Gates's entry into the art pottery field. Over the years he undertook several experiments in glazes and forms, with some pieces registered as early as 1895. In 1901, he introduced a line of art pottery he called Teco Ware, derived from Terra Cotta, the name of the town in which the pottery was located.

Teco Ware was produced in molds, which Gates, the practical businessman, saw as being essential for the viability of the line. Gates did much of the initial design, but also drew upon the talents of other artists and architects. They included F. Albert, W. J. Dodd, Blanche Ostertog, and Max Dunning.

Early glazes included browns, buff, and various shades of red. In 1904 a matte green glaze was added, similar to those of other potteries and advertised as a "cool, peaceful, healthful color—a tone not easily classified." This green became the predominant color in the Teco line for nearly a decade. As demand for the green began to fade in the 1910s, Gates introduced other colors, including brown, yellow, blue, rose, grey, purple, and other green tones. By 1911 there were over 500 designs in the Teco line.

The production of Teco Ware ended in the early 1920s. The company was sold to George A. Berry in 1929, and the name was changed.

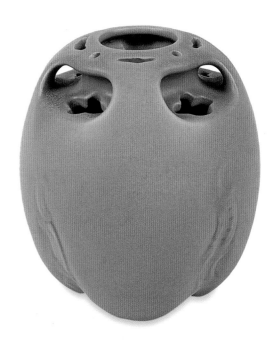

Teco vase. 6" h. $3,800. *Courtesy of Circa 1910 Antiques, Los Angeles.*

Teco frog bowl. 6.5", $1,195. *Courtesy of Olde City Mission, Philadelphia.*

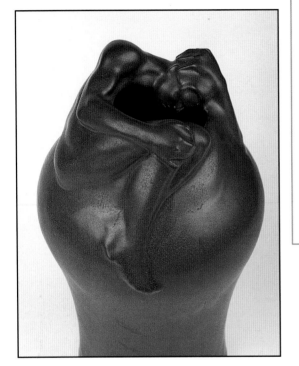

Van Briggle Pottery
Colorado Springs, Colorado, 1899–present

Artus Van Briggle was one of many young artists of the Art Academy of Cincinnati to go to work for Rookwood. He joined the company in 1887 and by 1894 had attained the status of senior artist. Rookwood sent him to Paris to study at the Académie Julian. There he met a fellow artist who later became his wife, Anne, to whom he became engaged in 1895. In 1896 he returned to Rookwood and spent the next three years as an underglaze artist and experimented with a new matte glaze. In 1899, suffering from tuberculosis, he was forced to seek a healthier climate. With Maria Nichols Storer's financial assistance he opened a pottery in Colorado Springs, Colorado, in 1899. His fiancée joined him in 1900 and by 1901 the Van Briggle Pottery was in full operation. Artus married Anne in 1902 and she worked with him at the pottery until his death in 1904 at the age of 35. Anne then took over the management of the pottery, overseeing a time of physical and creative growth. In 1908 she remarried, and in 1912 she left the pottery to resume her painting.

The pottery produced a variety of forms including glazed terra cotta architectural tiles, roof tiles, wall fountains, garden decorations, flower pots, and lamp bases.

The years that followed saw two changes in ownership and a serious fire, but the pottery continued. In 1920 it was purchased by I.F. and J.H. Lewis, who controlled it until 1969. The Van Briggle Pottery continues to this day.

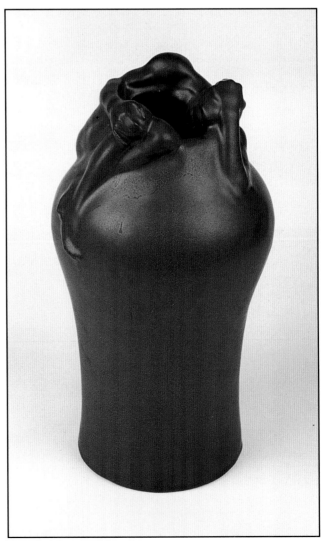

Van Briggle vase, "Despondency," 1915. Unusual in this glaze. 13" h. $22,000. *Courtesy of Circa 1910 Antiques, Los Angeles.*

Weller Pottery was founded in 1872 by Samuel A. Weller. It began in Fultonham, Ohio, moving to Zanesville in 1882, where it remained until it closed 1948. Art pottery was made from 1894. Among those who worked for Weller were Charles Babcock Upjohn, Frederick H. Rhead, and Jacques Sicard, whose Sicardo line is the most esteemed Weller art pottery line.

Large Weller vase. 14", $1,550.
Courtesy of Olde City Mission, Philadelphia.

Weller coppertone frog lawnsprinkler. 8", $2,200.
Courtesy of Olde City Mission, Philadelphia.

Weller coppertone. Left: vase, 10", $850: Right: candlesticks, 3", $295 pair. *Courtesy of Olde City Mission, Philadelphia.*

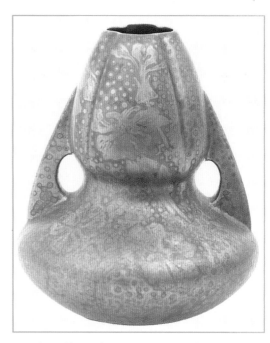

Sicardo Weller iridescent vase. 8" tall. $2,750.
Courtesy of Craftsman Auctions.

Weller vase. *Courtesy of Olde City Mission, Philadelphia.*

Wheatley Pottery Company
Cincinnati, Ohio, 1903-1910

Thomas J. Wheatley was born in 1853 and is remembered for his work in underglaze pottery. He received a patent for a method of applying underglaze colors, but was unable to enforce it. He helped form the Cincinnati Art Pottery in 1879 with Frank Huntington and began his own company, T.J. Wheatley & Company, in 1880. His association with the first and the operations of the second both ended in 1882. Wheatley opened a new venture, the Wheatley Pottery Company, in 1903. A fire in 1910 virtually ended the company's operations, though it continued in some fashion until 1927.

Wheatley wall pocket. 11", $750.
Courtesy of Olde City Mission, Philadelphia.

Three handled vase from an unknown southern pottery, probably
North Carolina. *Courtesy of Olde City Mission, Philadelphia.*

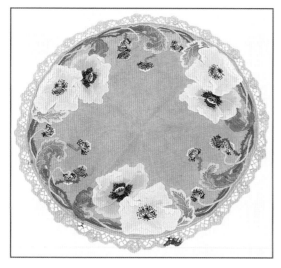

Embroidered table round. 36" diameter. $550. *Courtesy of Craftsman Auctions.*

While the English Arts & Crafts Movement produced wonderful textiles designed by William Morris and others and textiles were imported from Asia by Liberty & Co., few in America could afford these luxuries. Instead, embroidered goods, often in combination with stenciling, were

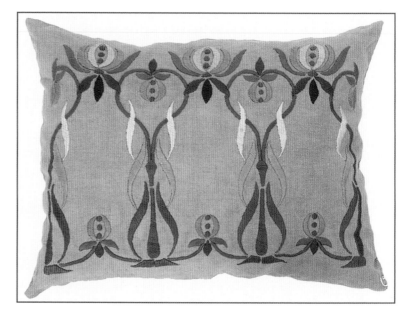

Linen pillow with iris embroidery. $600. *Courtesy of Craftsman Auctions.*

Linen pillow with embroidered and painted butterfly. $450. *Courtesy of Craftsman Auctions.*

Embroidered pillow. 18" x 18". $425. *Courtesy of Craftsman Auctions.*

available from a number of companies, including Stickley's United Crafts, in completed form or as kits to be completed by the homemaker herself. The works shown below are a testament to the creativity of the needleworker.

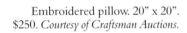

Embroidered pillow. 20" x 20". $250. *Courtesy of Craftsman Auctions.*

Embroidered pillow. 16" x 18" $350. *Courtesy of Craftsman Auctions.*

The ideals of the Arts & Crafts Movement have been carried on by craftspeople in each successive generation, even though the particular designs and aesthetics of the movement were out of fashion for many years. With its rediscovery and a renewed appreciation of its purposes, many designers have captured the spirit of Arts & Crafts designs in their own work. They have recovered the beauty of wood

and textile, the clean lines, the attention to detail, and always the striving for quality.

A few of these artisans are represented in the pages that follow. It is a only a sampling, for many more are engaged in these tasks than there is room to include here. As the reader will see, these new works keep alive the Arts & Crafts movement while bringing to it renewed creativity and vision.

Dennis and Denise Blankemeyer
American Furnishings Co.
Columbus, Ohio

Dennis and Denise Blankemeyer own the American Furnishings Co. in Columbus, Ohio. In addition to handling many of the finest contemporary artisans of Arts & Crafts inspired designs, they provide design services to clients around the country.

A Blankenmeyer-designed dining room. The fireplace acts as a warm focal point in the room, while the rug pulls it all together. *Courtesy of American Furnishings Co. Photo copyright © 2000 by Brad Feinknopf and used with permission.*

The Blankemeyer kitchens have all the modern conveniences for food preparation while preserving the warmth and hospitality of the Arts & Crafts style. *Courtesy of American Furnishings Co. Photo copyright © 2000 by Brad Feinknopf and used with permission.*

Though not emphasized in this volume, stained glass was a welcomed part of many Arts and Crafts homes. Here Dennis and Denise use it effectively at the landing of a beautiful oak staircase. *Courtesy of American Furnishings Co. Photo copyright © 2000 by Brad Feinknopf and used with permission.*

Beyond the home, Arts & Crafts design works well in the board room. This large conference table and chairs brings a sense of seriousness to the proceedings that take place around it. *Courtesy of American Furnishings Co. Photo copyright © 2000 by Brad Feinknopf and used with permission.*

David B. Hellman and Associates
Watertown, Massachusetts

David Hellman furniture is created to be both beautiful and useful. Incorporating the designs of brothers Charles and Henry Greene, the influential Arts & Crafts architects from Pasadena, California, each piece is a decorative tour de force. In awe of the Greene & Greene cabinetmakers under Peter and John Hall, David tries to put as much care and quality into each piece. David received his training at the North Bennet Street School in Boston in 1989 and has established his studio in Watertown, Massachusetts.

The Hellman mahogany and ebony "Signature Rocker" with pierced center splat. *Courtesy of David B. Hellman and Associates.*

"Gamble Rocker" in mahogany and ebony based on an example from the Gamble House, Pasadena, California. It is flanked by two "Thorsen" side tables with pierced aprons, based on a design from the Thorsen House in Berkeley, California. 42" x 26.5" x 37". *Courtesy of David B. Hellman and Associates.*

Close-up of the crest rail of Gamble Rocker showing the raised ebony pegs. *Courtesy of David B. Hellman and Associates.*

A pair of "Blacker Arm Chairs" in mahogany and ebony, based on originals in Greene & Greene's Blacker House, Pasadena, California. 34" x 24" x 22.5". *Courtesy of David B. Hellman and Associates.*

Quartersawn old-growth oak clock with through-tenon construction. 89" x 37" x 16.5". *Courtesy of David B. Hellman and Associates.*

The "Thorsen Dining Table" in mahogany and ebony. This round extension table has with chairs based on a sketch by Charles Greene, but never built. Table: 54" d. which extends to 114" using three leaves. *Courtesy of David B. Hellman and Associates.*

Mahogany and ebony "Gamble Table" with two drawers. Its original is in the entry hall of the Gamble House. 34" x 60" x 22". *Courtesy of David B. Hellman and Associates.*

Maple costumer based on one from the Robinson House in Pasadena, California. *Courtesy of David B. Hellman and Associates.*

Mahogany and ebony "Bolton Chair," a tall-back entry hall chair. *Courtesy of David B. Hellman and Associates.*

Craig McIlwain
Black Swamp Handcraft
Maumee, Ohio

Craig McIlwain was a third generation antiques dealer before he began to create his beautiful Arts & Crafts furniture. He learned much about how furniture was made and finished from the time he spent restoring antiques. About fifteen years ago he a bought a Limbert sideboard at auction and was hooked on the style. As pieces became less and less available he began to create pieces in the Arts & Crafts style He is a one man show, doing everything from design, to wood selection, to finishing in his Maumee shop.

Coffee table with two drawers. *Courtesy of Black Swamp Handcraft.*

Tabourets and stands. *Courtesy of Black Swamp Handcraft.*

Oak china cabinet with leaded glass doors above and oak cabinetry below. The hardware is hammered copper. This is based on an early, rare Gustav Stickley design. *Courtesy of Black Swamp Handcraft.*

Queen bed. *Courtesy of Black Swamp Handcraft.*

Armoire with cupboard at top and four drawers below. Shown
closed and open. *Courtesy of Black Swamp Handcraft.*

Eleven drawer stepped triple dresser. *Courtesy of Black Swamp Handcraft.*

Mirrored dresser with two drawers over two. *Courtesy of Black Swamp Handcraft.*

D-handle bookcase with a v-trough shelf above and a flat shelf below. *Courtesy of Huston & Sons.*

Huston & Sons
Midvale, Utah

Gordon Huston has been building Arts and Crafts furniture for more than ten years. He began soon after he and his wife moved into a small empty bungalow. While shopping to furnish the house, he realized that he could build better furniture himself than what he could afford to buy. So instead of furniture, he bought tools, set up a small shop in the garage, and began building furniture for his home. Soon he was building pieces for others who saw his work and asked for similar pieces for their homes. In 1998 he turned to furniture building full time and established J.G. Huston and Sons. Since that time the company has sought and completed private commissions, and worked to create a small line of hand-crafted Arts and Crafts furniture.

This oak magazine stand is faithful to the spirit of Gustav Stickley's original. It stands 43 inches high. *Courtesy of Huston & Sons.*

Another Stickley-inspired piece is this screen of oak and fabric. The wooden panels are joined with butterfly dovetails. Mortise and tenon joinery is used throughout. The height is 60 inches and the overall width is 60 inches. *Courtesy of Huston & Sons.*

Probst Furniture Makers
Hamlin, West Virginia

James Probst worked for several years as a carpenter and cabinet maker before turning to woodworking as a profession in 1988. All his work is handcrafted from Appalachian hardwoods. The Otto series reflects draws upon the Arts & Crafts Movement and the Shaker workshops...two design traditions that are not dissimilar.

A sidechair in cherry with ebonized cherry details. *Courtesy of Probst Furniture Makers.*

A closer look at the nightstand, this time in cherry with ebonized details. *Courtesy of Probst Furniture Makers.*

This is a queen-sized bed in walnut with butternut details. Also seen are matching stands and a bookshelf. *Courtesy of Probst Furniture Makers.*

Flat Rock Furniture
Waldreon, Indiana

Falt Rock Furniture was started by Van McQueen in 1986 to manufacture the rustic hickory furniture. While popular in the late 19th and early 20th centuries the last manufacturer had closed its doors in the late 1960s. The quality and beauty of Flat Rock's work and a rekindled and growing interest in rustic furniture has led to rapid growth of Flat Rock, with the original plant in Waldron, Indiana, and a more recent plant opened in Tyner, Kentucky in 1999. Flat Rock produces hickory furniture for both the home and commercial spaces.

The Indiana tradition of hickory furniture is kept alive by Flat Rock Furniture, which was founded in 1986. This elegant dining room scene includes armchairs (44" x 24" x 24"), sides chairs (44" x 20" x 22"), a dining table (30" x 76" x 40"), a side board (34" x 64" x 19"), an entertainment cabinet (72" x 45" x 22"), and a mirror (50" x 38"). *Courtesy of Flat Rock Furniture.*

For the living room Flat Rock makes the Loft Sofa (29" x 84" x 44"), the Loft Chair (29" x 42" x 44"), a tray table (23" x 48" x 24"), and a Parlor Table (29" x 32" x 32"). *Courtesy of Flat Rock Furniture.*

The bedroom has a beautiful queen bed, nightstand, and six drawer dresser with mirror. *Courtesy of Flat Rock Furniture.*

John Lomas
Cotswold Furniture Makers
Whitig, Vermont

The designs of John Lomas are influenced by the Arts & Crafts Movement in the Cotswolds of England and by the American Shakers. Trained in London, England, he eventually brought his studio and salesroom to a converted dairy barn south of Middlebury, Vermont. There he designs furniture that is "pleasing to the touch, gentle on the eye...fits harmoniously into any setting without dominating it"...and will give pleasure to its owners "for as long as they live."

Panelled bed in cherry with walnut detailing and footrail. *Courtesy of Cotswold Furniture Makers.*

Spindle Bed in cherry and walnut. *Courtesy of Cotswold Furniture Makers.*

Sapperton nine-drawer dresser. *Courtesy of Cotswold Furniture Makers.*

Chalford dining chairs. *Courtesy of Cotswold Furniture Makers.*

Custom pedestal table. *Courtesy of Cotswold Furniture Makers.*

Computer desk.
Courtesy of Cotswold Furniture Makers.

Gloucester table. *Courtesy of Cotswold Furniture Makers.*

**Jaeger & Ernst, Cabinetmakers
Barboursville, Virginia**

Jaeger & Ernst is a small classical cabinetmaker's shop specializing in design and craftsmanship in the Arts & Crafts tradition. They create beautiful, useful, and enduring interiors and furniture.

A Greene and Greene-style shedua server, designed as part of a dining room set. It is made of shedua and ebony with drawers of oak. 36" x 72" x 20". *Courtesy of Jaeger & Ernst.*

Close up of the cabinet work.

A Greene and Greene-inspired kitchen, designed and installed by Jaeger & Ernst. The cabinetry is cherry with granite tops. *Courtesy of Jaeger & Ernst.*

Arched server in koa with ebony accents and oak drawer. It melds design concepts from several G. Stickley pieces. 36" x 60" x 20" *Courtesy of Jaeger & Ernst.*

This curly cherry dresser draws its inspiration from Rennie Macintosh interpreted for today. 40" x 57" x 22". *Courtesy of Jaeger & Ernst.*

The "New American Chair" fits equally well in a bungalow and in a contemporary interior. 38" x 19" x 18". *Courtesy of Jaeger & Ernst.*

Shedua Greene and Greene-style chairs. Each has sixty ebony pegs adding both beauty and strength. 46" x 22" x 19". A sidechair and armchair. *Courtesy of Jaeger & Ernst.*

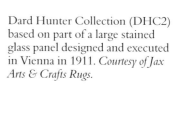

Del & Jerri Martin
Jax Arts & Crafts Rugs
Berea, Kentucky

Del Martin, a salesman in an oriental rug shop, stopped by the Roycroft campus in August of 1991, at the insistence of his friend Dard Hunter III. It changed the direction of his life. With a new interest in the Arts & Crafts Movement, he began to look at the production of rug manufacturers, but while there were plenty of attempts, noone was producing rugs that were true to the designs of the Arts & Crafts masters.

Being passionate about it, he started Jax Rugs in March, 1995. He developed three designs based on Dard Hunter illustrations and sent them to Nepal to be manufactured by hand.

Gustav Stickley scroll drugget design. Produced in 3' x 6' and 6'x 9' sizes

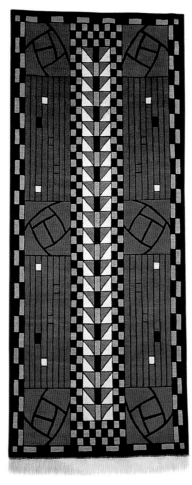

Dard Hunter Collection (DHC2) based on part of a large stained glass panel designed and executed in Vienna in 1911. *Courtesy of Jax Arts & Crafts Rugs.*

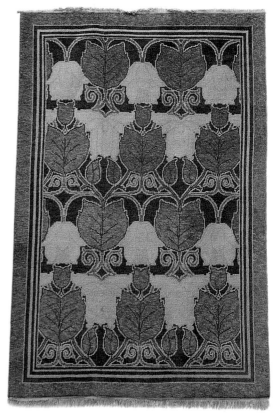

Magnolia Donegal rug (JV-1). The design was offered in a Stickley catalog. Made in Nepal, available in 6' x 9', 8' x 10', and 9' x 12'. *Courtesy of Jax Arts & Crafts Rugs.*

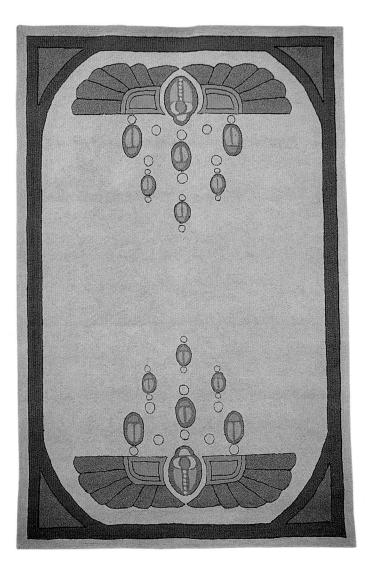

Scarab, available in 3'6" x 5'6", 5'6" x 8'6", 2'7" x 8', and 2'7" x 10'. *Courtesy of Jax Arts & Crafts Rugs.*

Gustav Stickley Donegal (JV-5) with a "wave" design attributed to C.F.A. Voysey. It is pictured in numerous illustrations in "The Craftsman" (Gustav Stickley) as well as in Stickley catalogues. Made in Nepal in 6' x 9' and 8' x 10'. *Courtesy of Jax Arts & Crafts Rugs.*

Waterlily (JV-4) runner in an unnamed design is attributed to C.F.A. Voysey. There are stylistic similarities between this ca.1903 design and a fragment of a known Voysey carpet in the Victoria and Albert Museum, London. *Courtesy of Jax Arts & Crafts Rugs.*

The Glenmure (JV-6) design taken from a rare antique example shown elsewhere in this book. It is attributed to Voysey because of similarities to his early style. Made in Nepal and available in 6' x 9' and 8' x 10' sizes. *Courtesy of Jax Arts & Crafts Rugs.*

David E. Berman
Trustworh Studios
Plymouth, Massachusetts

David Berman and Trustworth Studios work with wood, metal, paint and textiles, translating them into furniture and accessories, lighting, artwork, and needlework for both large and small utilitarian purposes. The influence of of Voysey and the English Arts & Crafts Movement is evident in Trustworthy's creative output, both in the pieces shown here and in major interior designs in the United States, England, and Europe.

Voysey Chair 1, an armchair with pierced backsplat, available with rush or leather seat. 40.5" h. x 25" w. It also is made as a sidechair. *Courtesy of Trustworth Studios.*

Voysey Chair 2, a highback armchair available with rush or leather seat. 54" h. x 25" w. *Courtesy of Trustworth Studios.*

Voysey Table, a gateleg table with a round top and six hexagonal tapered legs, supported by arched buttresses to the center. 26" h. x 30" d. (10" deep when closed). *Courtesy of Trustworth Studios.*

Voysey Garden Gnome Chair, 29" d. x
31" w. x 61" h. *Courtesy of Trustworth
Studios.*

Owl and Spider light, oak, copper, and glass. 18" x 18"
x 12" with a 20.5" canopy. *Courtesy of Trustworth Studios.*

Oak, copper, and mica round light derived from
a Voysey pierced metalwork lantern. 13.5" d.,
17" canopy. *Courtesy of Trustworth Studios.*

V. Michael Ashford
Evergreen Studios
Olympia, Washington

Evergreen Studios was started by V. Michael Ashford in 1988, as a one-man shop. They create the lighting items that appear in their catalog, as well a full custom service. While their work is primarily in copper, they also use wrought iron when warranted. The designs emulate Van Erp, Roycroft, and Gustav Stickley. All the work is hammered by hand.

Six-panel uplighter chandelier with amber mica, no. 1033. *Courtesy of Evergreen Studios. Photo by David Stein.*

Bullet table lamp, no. 910 custom. *Courtesy of Evergreen Studios. Photo by David McNamee.*

Four pendant chandelier with amber mica, no. 1014. *Courtesy of Evergreen Studios. Photo by David Stein.*

Van Erp "Flat Top" table lamp with amber mica, no. 916. *Courtesy of Evergreen Studios. Photo by David McNamee.*

"Warty" table lamp with dark amber mica, no. 911. *Courtesy of Evergreen Studios. Photo by David McNamee.*

Custom dining room fixture with four pendants. *Courtesy of Evergreen Studios. Photo by David McNamee.*

Cherry Tree Design
Bozeman, Montana

Cherry Tree Design offers a line of fine hardwood lighting that feature Pacific Rim, Traditional, Craftsman, and Contemporary styling. Each lamp and lighting fixture is made in the USA using the finest quality of American hardwoods and facings available. All products feature furniture quality finishes, paired wtih exceptional joinery and craftsman techniques.

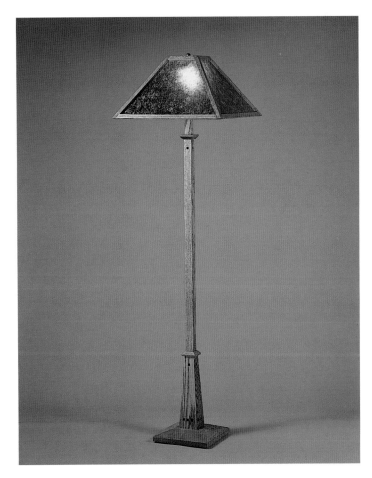

Mission table lamp, no. L-71. 25" x 16". Oak base and amber mica shade. *Courtesy of Cherry Tree Design.*

Mission floor lamp, no. L-70. 62" x 18". Oak base and amber mica shade. *Courtesy of Cherry Tree Design.*

Bungalow table lamp, L-81. 25" x 16". Oak base with iridescent shade. *Courtesy of Cherry Tree Design.*

Craftsman Three Light
Chandelier, L-36. 36"
wide with 11.5" high
fixtures. *Courtesy of
Cherry Tree Design.*

Gallery Table Lamp, L-41.
16" x 25" h. *Courtesy of
Cherry Tree Design.*

Gallery Floor Lamp, L-40. 18"
x 62" h. *Courtesy of Cherry Tree
Design.*

Mica Lamp Company
Glendale, California

Hannes Schachtner and Ralph Ribicic conceived of Mica Lamps in 1992. They shared a passion for the work of the Arts & Crafts era metalsmiths. Hans brought the skills of a coppersmith and Ralph brought the experience of many years in lighting manufacturing. Their lamps are made of solid copper, assembled iwth hand driven copper rivets. The shades are made in the same manner as the originals. Each piece is individually numbered.

Pasadena lamp with oak base and mica shade with pierced copper frame, no. 041. 23" x 14". *Courtesy of Mica Lamps.*

Large Trumpet lamp, no. 014. Copper base with mica shade. 24" x 20" d. *Courtesy of Mica Lamps.*

Large Onion Lamp. Copper base with mica shade, no. 013. 24" x 20" d. *Courtesy of Mica Lamps.*

Library Lamp, no. 040. Oak base with mica shade. 20" x 24". *Courtesy of Mica Lamps.*

Karl Barry
New York

Karl Barry has been creating beautiful lighting for over 25 years in the Arts & Crafts spirit.

Karl Barry bronze and slag glass lamp. 16.5" x 12" x 12". *Courtesy of Circa 1910 Antiques, Los Angeles.*

Jerome Venneman Pottery
Oakland, California

Jerome Venneman was introduced to Arts & Crafts pottery in the late 1970s, and began to collect it. The love affair grew, until he decided to try his hand at making pottery himself. Although he did not set out to work in the Arts & Crafts style, after many years of experimenting with glaze development and incised designs he began to produce pottery that were true to the Arts & Crafts philosophy. In truth many influences find their way into his work including Art Nouveau, Secession, and Southwest American Indian designs. The result is a pottery that is unique and expressive of the artist's own vision.

Secession, no. 35, To Be Blue glaze. *Courtesy of Jerome Venneman Pottery.*

Summer Storm, no. 36, Sierra Green glaze. *Courtesy of Jerome Venneman Pottery.*

245

Rose, no. 3, Sierra Green glaze.
Courtesy of Jerome Venneman Pottery.

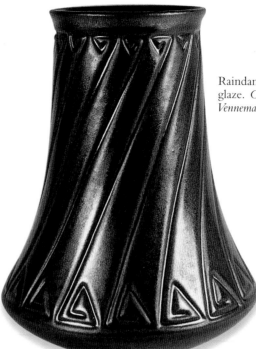

Raindance, no. 49, Old Copper glaze. *Courtesy of Jerome Venneman Pottery.*

Glasgow, no. 37, Sierra Gold glaze.
Courtesy of Jerome Venneman Pottery.

Sunflower, no. 28. *Courtesy of Jerome Venneman Pottery.*

Arrowhead, no. 52, Tan Granite glaze. *Courtesy of Jerome Venneman Pottery.*

Yarrow, no 2. *Courtesy of Jerome Venneman Pottery.*

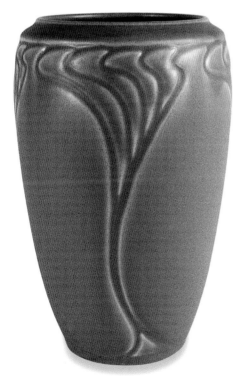

Big Sur, no. 1, Sierra Green glaze *Courtesy of Jerome Venneman Pottery.*

Tumbleweed, no. 8, Old Copper glaze. *Courtesy of Jerome Venneman Pottery.*

Karim and Nawal Motawi
Motawi Tileworks
Ann Arbor Michigan

Motawi Tileworks is a ceramic art tile studio specializing in the Arts & Crafts style. It produces tiles for installation as well as individual art pieces. It is owned by founder and designer Nawal Motawi and her brother, Karim Motawi, who work with a dozen tile production and design artisans. The tiles are made by the press mold method, and are then waxed and hand-glazed using a variety of techniques.

Fireplace surround using a combination of field tiles and relief tiles. The relief tiles are no. 6606, Art Nouveau in the upper corners and no. 6608, Art Nouveau in the top center. *Courtesy of Motawi Tileworks.*

Fireplace surround including field and relief tiles. Some of those included are owl, art nouveau, cat, stag, celtic, and celtic knot. *Courtesy of Motawi Tileworks.*

Owl, no. 4411, 4" x 4"

"Medallion" polychrome tile with cat, dog, rabbit and stag around the center and doves in the corners, based on medieval design. 8" x 8". *Courtesy of Motawi Tileworks.*

Leaves & Berries relief tile, no. 8803. 8" x 8". *Courtesy of Motawi Tileworks.*

Dutura series, colorway C. This series comes in a choice of nine colorways and four sizes. 6" x 6". *Courtesy of Motawi Tileworks.*

Datura series, colorway K. 8"
x 8". *Courtesy of Motawi
Tileworks.*

Datura, colorway G. 3" x 3".
Courtesy of Motawi Tileworks.

Arts and Crafts Landscape, polychrome glaze. overall
size 6" x 12". *Courtesy of Motawi Tileworks.*

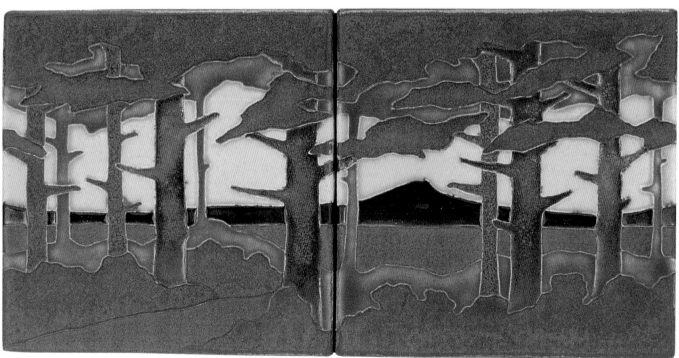

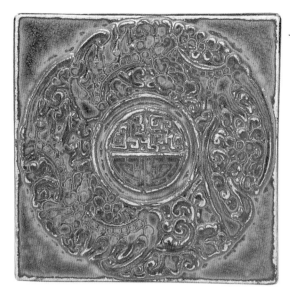

Japan, no. 6620. 6" x 6"

Swirl series, no. 6660 in the
Turquoise colorway. 6" x 6".
Courtesy of Motawi Tileworks.

Fireplace surround using 6" x 6" relief tiles mixed
with field and geometric tiles. The relief tiles are
Rabbit, no. 6601, Stag, no. 6604, Dog, no. 6602, and
Griffin-L, no. 6611. *Courtesy of Motawi Tileworks.*

Fish series, no. 8817, Green
Fish colorway. 8" x 8".
Courtesy of Motawi Tileworks.

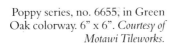

Poppy series, no. 6655, in Green
Oak colorway. 6" x 6". *Courtesy of
Motawi Tileworks.*

Landscape series. Twenty-one tile panel of a forest scene, measuring 18"
x 42". This is being developed into a 30" tall version. The pattern can be
repeated for a continuous panel. *Courtesy of Motawi Tileworks.*

Ephraim Faience Art Pottery
Deerfield, Wisconsin

Ephraim Pottery began in 1996, when Kevin Hicks, a potter, and Scott Draves, a decorator, grew frustrated with the demands of mass production pottery, and sought a more rewarding of practicing their art. Their ideals have become reality and their creations have found wide acceptance.

More Ephraim pots. *Courtesy of Ephraim Faience Art Pottery.*

A selection of Ephraim pots. *Courtesy of Ephraim Faience Art Pottery.*

New Spring vase in the style of the Saturday Evening Girls. 8.75" x 4.5". *Courtesy of Ephraim Faience Art Pottery.*

Rhinoceros Beetle vase with a "fall maple leaf curdle glaze." 5" x 7.25". *Courtesy of Ephraim Faience Art Pottery.*

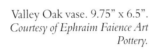

Valley Oak vase. 9.75" x 6.5". *Courtesy of Ephraim Faience Art Pottery.*

Pacific Eucalyptus vase. 11.5" x 4.5". *Courtesy of Ephraim Faience Art Pottery.*

Cottonwood Grove vases in the Saturday Evening Girls style. 5.25" x 5". *Courtesy of Ephraim Faience Art Pottery.*

BIBLIOGRAPHY

Altman, Seymour and Violet. *The Book of Buffalo Pottery.* Atglen, PA: Schiffer Publishing, Ltd., 1987

Anderson, Timothy J., Eurdorah M. Moore, and Robert W. Winter. *California Design 1910.* Salt Lake City: Peregrine Smith Books, 1980 (reprint of the 1974 edition published by California Design Publications, Pasadena, CA)

Cathers, David M. *Furniture of the American Arts and Crafts Movement.* New York: Turn of the Century Editions, 1996.

Congdon-Martin, Douglas. Arts & Crafts: the California Home. Atglen, Pennsylvania: Schiffer Publishing, Ltd., 1998.

Current, Karen. *Greene & Greene: Architects in the Residential Style.* Fort Worth: Amon Carter Museum of Western Art, 1974.

Gilborn, Craig. *Adirondack Furniture and the Rustic Tradition.* New York: Harry N. Abrams, Inc. 1987.

Hamilton, Charles F. *Roycroft Collectibles.* New York: A.S. Barnes & Company, 1980.

Henzke, Lucile. *Art Pottery in America.* Atglen, PA: Schiffer Publishing Ltd., 1996.

Johnson, Bruce. *The Official Identification and Price Guide to Arts and Crafts: The Early Modernist Movement in American Decorative Arts: 1894-1923.* New York: House of Collectibles, 1992.

Kardon, Janet, general editor. *The Ideal Home 1900-1920: the History of Twentieth Century Craft in America.* New York: Harry N. Abrams, Incorporated, 1993.

Kovel, Ralph and Terry. *Kovel's American Art Pottery.* New York: Crown Publishers, Inc. 1993.

Limbert, Charles, and Company. *Limbert Arts and Crafts Furniture: The Complete 1903 Catalog.* New York: Dover Publications, Inc., 1992.

Makinson, Randell L. *Greene & Greene: Architecture as a Fine Art.* Salt Lake City: Peregrine Smith, Inc., 1977.

Mayer, Barbara. *In the Arts & Crafts Style.* San Francisco: Chronicle Books, 1993.

McConnell, Kevin. *Heintz Art Metal: Silver-On-Bronze Wares.* Atglen, PA: Schiffer Publishing, Ltd., 1990.

_____. *Roycroft Art Metal,* 2nd Edition. Atglen, PA: Schiffer Publishing, Ltd., 1990.

_____. *More Roycroft Art Metal.* Atglen, PA: Schiffer Publishing, Ltd. 1995.

Parry, Linda. *William Morris.* New York: Harry N. Abrams, 1996.

Poesch, Jessie. *Newcomb Pottery.* Atglen, PA: Schiffer Publishing, Ltd., 1984.

Rago, David. *American Art Pottery.* New York: Knickerbocker Press, 1997.

Royka, Paul. *Mission Furniture: From the American Arts & Crafts Movement.*

Atglen, PA: Schiffer Publishing, Ltd., 1997.

_____. *Fireworks: New England Art Pottery of the Arts & Crafts Movement.* Atglen, PA: Schiffer Publishing, Ltd., 1997.

Roycrofters, The. *Roycroft Furniture Catalog,* 1906. New York: Dover Publications Inc., 1994.

Skinner, Tina, ed. *American Wooden Chairs, 1895-1908.* Atglen, Pennsylvania: Schiffer Publishing, Ltd. 19997.

Stickley, Gustav. *Craftsman Fabrics and Needlework (reprinted 1995). Milwaukee: Razmataz Press, 1995 (reprint).*

_____.*Craftsman Homes: Mission-Style Homes and Furnishings of the American Arts and Crafts Movement.* New York: Random House, 1995 (reprint)

_____.*Craftsman Homes: Architecture and Furnishings of the American Arts and Crafts Movement.* New York: Dover Publications Inc., 1979.

_____.*The 1912 and 1915 Gustav Stickley Craftsman Furniture Catalogs.* New York: The Athenaeum of Philadelphia and Dover Publications, Inc., 1991. (Reprint)

_____. *Stickley Craftsman Furniture Catalogs.* New York: Dover Publications Inc., 1979. (Reprint)

Stickley, L. & J.G. Early L. & J.G. *Stickley Furniture: From Onondaga Shops to Handcraft.* New York: Dover Publications Inc., 1992. (Reprint)

Trapp, Kenneth R. *The Arts and Crafts Movement in California: Living the Good Life.* The Oakland Museum. New York: Abbeville Press, 1993.

Winter, Robert. *The California Bungalow.* Los Angeles: Hennessey & Ingalls, 1980.

Wissinger, Joana. *Arts and Crafts: Pottery and Ceramics.* San Francisco: Chronicle Books, 1994.